Buddhist Economics

About the Author

Venerable Prayudh Payutto was born in 1939 in Suphanburi Province in Central Thailand, and became a novice at the age of 13. While still a novice, he completed the highest grade of Pali examinations in Thailand, an achievement for which he was honored with the rare distinction of ordination as a monk under royal patronage in 1961. After completing a degree in Buddhist studies from Mahachulalongkorn Buddhist University and a Higher certificate in Education, he served for a time as Deputy Secretary General of the University and as Abbot of Wat Prapirane in Bangkok. He has spent time lecturing on Buddhism and Thai culture at Swarthmore College, Harvard University and other educational institutions in the U.S., and has received Honorary Degrees in Buddhist Studies, Philosophy, Education and Linguistics from the major Universities in Bangkok. In 1994 he was the winner of the UNESCO prize for Peace Education in honor of his services in that field.

Buddhist Economics

A Middle Way for the market place

By

Ven. P. A. Payutto

Translated by Dhammavijaya and Bruce Evans
Compiled by Bruce Evans and Jourdan Arenson

BUDDHADHAMMA FOUNDATION
BANGKOK THAILAND

Buddhist Economics, a Middle Way for the market place
P. A. Payutto

ISBN : 974-89070-3-1

First Printed as *Buddhist Economics* : May, 1992
Second Edition (Revised and Enlarged): July, 1994
Third Impression : August 1996
Fourth Impression : January 1997
Fifth Impression : July 1998

Published by:
Buddhadhamma Foundation
87/126 Tesabahl Songkroh Rd., Lad Yao,
Chatuchak, Bangkok 10900, THAILAND.
Tel : (66–2) 589-9012, 580-2719
Fax : (66–2) 954-4791

Printed at:
SAHADHAMMIKA LTD.,
54/67-68, 71-72 Jaran Sanitwong 12, Jaran Sanitwong Rd,
Tha Phra, Bangkok Yai, Bangkok 10700, THAILAND.
Tel : (66–2) 412-5891, 412-5887
Fax : (66-2) 412-3087

Cover Design: *Panya Vijinthanasarn*

Contents

Translator's Foreword (First Edition)

These days Buddhist meditation techniques are well-known in the West and Buddhist insights into the human condition are, at least in academic circles, exerting a growing influence. Unfortunately the popular image of Buddhism is often an overly-austere one and many people still consider it to teach a denial or escape from worldly concerns into a private, hermetic realm of bliss. However, if we take the trouble to go to the words of the Buddha himself, we find a full and rich teaching encompassing every aspect of human life, with a great deal of practical advice on how to live with integrity, wisdom and peace in the midst of a confusing world. Perhaps it is time for such teaching to be more widely disseminated.

In this small volume, Venerable Dhammapitaka (P. A. Payutto) offers a Buddhist perspective on the subject of economics. While not seeking to present a comprehensive Buddhist economic theory, he provides many tools for reflection, ways of looking at economic questions based on a considered appreciation of the way things are, the way we are. I hope that making this work available in English may go at least a short way towards resolving what has been called the current 'impasse of economics,' and to awaken readers to the wide-reaching contemporary relevance of the timeless truths that the Buddha discovered and shared with us.

Dhammavijaya
May, 1992

Author's preface

It is well known that the study of economics has up till now avoided questions of moral values and considerations of ethics, which are abstract qualities. However, it is becoming obvious that in order to solve the problems that confront us in the world today it will be necessary to take into consideration both concrete and abstract factors, and as such it is impossible to avoid the subject of moral values. If the study of economics is to play any part in the solution of our problems, it can no longer evade the subject of ethics. Nowadays environmental factors are taken into account both in economic transactions and in solving economic problems, and the need for ethics in addressing the problem of conservation and the environment is becoming more and more apparent.

In fact, economics is one "science" which most clearly integrates the concrete and the abstract. It is the realm in which abstract human values interact most palpably with the material world. If economists were to stop evading the issue of moral values, they would be in a better position to influence the world in a fundamental way and to provide solutions to the problems of humanity and the world at large. Ideally, economics should play a part in providing mankind with opportunities for real individual and social growth rather than simply being a tool for catering to selfish needs and feeding contention in society, and, on a broader scale, creating imbalance and insecurity within the whole global structure with its innumerable ecosystems.

I would like to express my appreciation to Dhammavijaya, who translated the first Thai edition of Buddhist Economics, which was published by the Buddhadhamma Foundation in August, 1988, into English. His translation was published in May, 1992, and that edition has served as the basis for the second edition. I would like to also express my thanks to Bruce Evans and Jourdan Arenson, who were inspired enough to compile and translate further sources of teachings on Buddhist economics from among my talks and writings published in both Thai and English, and thus produce a more comprehensive treatment of the subject. I would also like to express my appreciation to Khun Yongyuth Thanapura and the Buddhadhamma Foundation who, as with the First Edition, have seen the printing through to completion.

Ven. P. A. Payutto
July, 1994

Introduction

The Spiritual Approach to Economics

Our libraries are full of books offering well-reasoned, logical formulas for the ideal society. Two thousand years ago, Plato, in *The Republic*, wrote one of the first essays on politics and started a search for an ideal society which has continued to the present day. Plato built his ideal society on the assumption that early societies grew from a rational decision to secure well-being, but if we look at the course of history, can we say that rational thinking has truly been the guiding force in the evolution of civilization? The reader is invited to imagine the beginnings of human society: groups of stone age humans are huddled together in their caves, each looking with suspicion on the group in the next cave down. They are cold and hungry. Danger and darkness surround them. Suddenly one of them hits on a brilliant idea: "I know, let's create a society where we can trade and build hospitals and live in mutual well-being!"

Such a scenario is not likely. Early humans, and the first societies, were probably bound together more by their deep emotional needs for warmth and security than any rational planning. And over the millennia, our societies have evolved to a large extent at the directives of these emotional needs. To be sure, rational thinking has played some part in the process, but if we take an honest look at our so-called advanced society, we must admit that our needs for security today are not so different from the cave man's. While our societies are certainly more complex, the propelling force is still emotion, not reason.

If we are to honestly discuss economics, we must admit that emotional factors—fear and desire and the irrationality they generate— have a very powerful influence on the market place. Economic decisions—decisions about production, consumption and distribution—are made by people in their struggle to survive and prosper. For the most part, these decisions are motivated by an emotional urge for self-preservation.

There is nothing inherently bad about fear and irrationality; they are natural conditions that come with being human. Unfortunately, however, fear and desire drive us to our worst economic excesses. The forces of greed, exploitation and overconsumption seem to have overwhelmed our economies in recent decades. Our materialistic societies offer us little choice but to exploit and compete for survival in today's dog-eat-dog world. But at the same time, it is obvious that these forces are damaging our societies and ravaging our environment.

In the face of such problems, the science of economics adopts a rational approach. The job of economists is to devise well-reasoned models to help society rise above fear, greed and hatred. Rarely, however, do economists examine the basic question of fear and the emotional needs for security that drive human beings. As a result, their theoretical models remain rational solutions to largely irrational problems, and their economic ideals can only truly exist in books.

Perhaps a little idealism is not so harmful; but there is a danger to the purely rational approach. At its worst, it is used to rationalize our basest, most fear-ridden responses to the question of survival. We see this tendency in the corporate strategists, policy advisors and defence analysts who logically and convincingly argue that arms production is in our best interests. When rationalism turns a blind eye to the irrational, unseen irrational impulses are all the more likely to cloud our rationality.

The book you are reading takes a different approach—a spiritual approach. As such, it does not delve into the technical intricacies of economics. Instead it examines the fundamental fears, desires and emotions that motivate our economic activities. Of all the spiritual traditions, Buddhism is best suited to this task. As we shall see, the Buddhist teachings offer profound insights into the psychology of desire and the motivating forces of economic activity. These insights can lead to a liberating self-awareness that slowly dissolves the confusion between what is truly harmful and what is truly beneficial in production and consumption. This awareness is, in turn, the foundation for a mature ethics.

Truly rational decisions must be based on insight into the forces that make us irrational. When we understand the nature of desire, we see that it cannot be satisfied by all the riches in the world. When we understand the universality of fear, we find a natural compassion for all beings. Thus, the spiritual approach to economics leads not to models and theories, but to the vital forces that can truly benefit our world—wisdom, compassion and restraint.

In other words, the spiritual approach must be lived. This is not to say that one must embrace Buddhism and renounce the science of economics, because, in the larger scheme of things, the two are mutually supportive. In fact, one needn't be a Buddhist or an economist to practise Buddhist economics. One need only acknowledge the common thread that runs through life and seek to live in balance with the way things really are.

Bruce Evans and Jourdan Arenson

Chapter One

The Problem of Specialization

In a discussion of Buddhist economics, the first question that arises is whether such a thing actually exists, or whether it is even possible. The image of a Buddhist monk quietly walking on alms round does not readily come to mind as an economic activity for most people. Skyscrapers, shopping centres and the stock market would more accurately fit the bill. At present the economics that we are acquainted with is a Western one. When talking of economics or matters pertaining to it, we use a Western vocabulary and we think within the conceptual framework of Western economic theory. It is difficult to avoid these constraints when talking about a Buddhist economics. We might find ourselves in fact discussing Buddhism with the language and concepts of Western economics. Even so, in the course of this book, I hope to at least provide some Buddhist perspectives on things that can be usefully employed in economics.

While economic thinking has been in existence since the time of Plato and Aristotle, the study of economics has only really crystallized into a science in the industrial era. Like other sciences in this age of specialization, economics has become a narrow and rarefied discipline; an isolated, almost stunted, body of knowledge, having little to do with other disciplines or human activities.

Ideally, the sciences should provide solutions to the complex, interrelated problems that face humanity, but cut off as it is from other disciplines and the larger sphere of human activity, economics can do little to ease the ethical, social and environmental problems that face us today. And given the tremendous influence it exerts on our market-driven societies, narrow economic thinking may, in fact, be the primary cause of some of our most pressing social and environmental troubles.

Like other sciences, economics strives for objectivity. In the process, however, subjective values, such as ethics, are excluded. With no consideration of subjective, moral values, an economist may say, for instance, that a bottle of whiskey and a Chinese dinner have the same economic value, or that drinking in a night club contributes more to the economy than listening to a religious talk or volunteering for humanitarian work. These are truths according to economics.

But the objectivity of economics is shortsighted. Economists look at just one short phase of the natural causal process and single out the part that interests them, ignoring the wider ramifications. Thus, modern economists take no account of the ethical consequences of economic activity. Neither the vices associated with the frequenting of night clubs, nor the wisdom arising from listening to a religious teaching, are its concern.

But is it in fact desirable to look on economics as a science? Although many believe that science can save us from the perils of life, it has many limitations. Science shows only one side of the truth, that which concerns the material world. By only considering the material side of things, the science of economics is out of step with the overall truth of the way things are. Given that all things in this world are naturally interrelated and interconnected, it follows that human problems must also be interrelated and interconnected. One-sided scientific solutions are bound to fail, and the problems bound to spread.

Environmental degradation is the most obvious and dangerous consequence to our industrialized, specialized approach to solving problems. Environmental problems have become so pressing that people are now beginning to see how foolish it is to place their faith in individual, isolated disciplines that ignore the larger perspective. They are starting to look at human activities on a broader scale, to see the repercussions their actions have on personal lives, society, and the environment.

From a Buddhist perspective, economics cannot be separated from other branches of knowledge. Economics is rather one component of a concerted effort to remedy the problems of humanity; and an economics based on Buddhism, a "Buddhist economics," is therefore not so much a self-contained science, but one of a number of interdependent disciplines working in concert toward the common goal of social, individual and environmental well-being.

One of the first to integrate the Buddha's teachings with economics (and indeed to coin the phrase "Buddhist economics") was E. F. Schumacher in his book *Small is Beautiful.** In his essay on Buddhist economics, Mr. Schumacher looks to the Buddhist teaching of the Noble Eightfold Path to make his case. He affirms that the inclusion of the factor of Right Livelihood in the Eightfold Path, in other words the Buddhist way of life, indicates the necessity of a Buddhist economics. This is Mr. Schumacher's starting point.

Looking back, we can see that both the writing of *Small is Beautiful,* and the subsequent interest in Buddhist economics shown by some Western academics, took place in response to a crisis. Western academic disciplines and conceptual structures have reached a point which many feel to be a dead end, or if not, at least a turning point demanding new paradigms of thought and methodology. This has led many economists to rethink their isolated, specialized approach. The serious environmental reper-

* *Small is Beautiful, Economics as if People Mattered,* by E. F. Schumacher, first published by Blond & Briggs Ltd., London, 1973

cussions of rampant consumerism have compelled economists to develop more ecological awareness. Some even propose that all new students of economics incorporate basic ecology into their curriculum.

Mr. Schumacher's point that the existence of Right Livelihood as one of the factors of the Noble Eightfold Path necessitates a Buddhist economics has a number of implications. Firstly, it indicates the importance given to Right Livelihood (or economics) in Buddhism. Secondly, and conversely, it means that economics is taken to be merely one amongst a number of factors (traditionally eight) that comprise a right way of life, that is, one capable of solving the problems of life.

Specialization can be a great benefit as long as we don't lose sight of our common goal: as a specialized study, economics allows us to analyze with minute detail the causes and factors within economic activities. But it is a mistake to believe that any one discipline or field of learning can in itself solve all problems. In concert with other disciplines, however, economics can constitute a complete response to human suffering, and it is only by fully understanding the contributions and limitations of each discipline that we will be able to produce such a coordinated effort.

Unfortunately, as it stands, economics is grossly out of touch with the whole stream of causes and conditions that constitute reality. Economics, and indeed all the social sciences, are, after all, based on man-made or artificial truths. For example, according to natural laws, the action of digging the earth results in a hole. This is a fixed cause and effect relationship based on natural laws. However, the digging which results in a wage is a conventional truth based on a social agreement. Without the social agreement, the action of digging does not result in a wage. While economists scrutinize one isolated segment of the cause and effect process, the universe manifests itself in an inconceivably vast array of causes and conditions, actions and reactions. Focused as they are on the linear progression of the economic events that concern them, economists forget that nature unfolds in all directions. In nature, actions and results are not confined to isolated spheres. One action gives rise to results, which in turn becomes a cause for further results. Each result conditions further results. In this way, action and reaction are intertwined to form the vibrant fabric of causes and conditions that we perceive as reality. To understand reality, it is necessary to understand this process.

The Two Meanings of Dhamma

For many people, the term "Buddhist economics" may evoke the image of an ideal society where all economic activity—buying and selling, production and consumption—adheres to strict ethical standards. But such an idealized image, attractive as it may sound, does not convey the full depth of the Buddha's teachings. The Buddha's teachings point to *Dhamma*, or truth. In Buddhism the term Dhamma is used to convey different levels of truth, both relative truths and ultimate truth.

Those truths regarding ethical behavior—both on a personal day-to-day basis and in society—are called *cariyadhamma*. These are the truths related to matters of good and evil. Dhamma in its larger sense is *saccadhamma*, truth, or *sabhāvadhamma*, reality: it includes all things as they are and the laws by which they function. In this sense, Dhamma is used to describe the entire stream of causes and conditions, the process by which all things exist and function.

Unlike the narrower scope of *cariyadhamma*, which refers to isolated ethical considerations, *sabhāvadhamma* points to nature or reality itself, which is beyond concerns of good and evil. In this all-encompassing sense, Dhamma expresses the totality of natural conditions, that which the various branches of science seek to describe.

Thus, the Buddha's teachings give us more than just ethical guidelines for a virtuous life. His teachings offer a grand insight into the nature of reality. Given the twofold meaning of the term Dhamma, it follows that an economics inspired by the Dhamma would be both attuned to the grand sphere of causes and conditions and, at the same time, guided by the specific ethical teachings based on natural reality. In other words, Buddhist economists would not only consider the ethical values of economic activity, but also strive to understand reality and direct economic activity to be in harmony with "the way things are."

Ultimately, economics cannot be separated from Dhamma, because all the activities we associate with economics emerge from the Dhamma. Economics is just one part of a vast interconnected whole, subject to the same natural laws by which all things function. Dhamma describes the workings of this whole, the basic truth of all things, including economics. If economics is ignorant of the Dhamma—of the complex and dynamic process of causes-and-effects that constitutes reality—then it will be hard pressed to solve problems, much less produce the benefits to which it aims.

Yet this is precisely the trouble with modern economic thinking. Lacking any holistic, comprehensive insight and limited by the narrowness of their specialized view, economists single out one isolated portion of the stream of conditions and fail to consider results beyond that point. An example: there exists a demand for a commodity, such as whiskey. The demand is supplied by production—growing grain and distilling it into liquor. The whiskey is then put on the market and then purchased and consumed. When it is consumed, demand is satisfied. Modern economic thinking stops here, at the satisfaction of the demand. There is no investigation of what happens after the demand is satisfied.

By contrast, an economics inspired by Dhamma would be concerned with how economic activities influence the entire process of causes and conditions. While modern economics confines its regard to events within its specialized sphere, Buddhist economics would investigate how a given economic activity affects the three interconnected spheres of human existence: the individual, society, and nature or the environment. In the case of the demand for a commodity such as whiskey, we would have to ask ourselves how liquor production affects the ecology and how its consumption affects the individual and society.

These are largely ethical considerations and this brings us back to the more specialized meaning of Dhamma, that relating to matters of good and evil. It is said in the Buddhist scriptures that good actions lead to good results and bad actions lead to bad results. All of the Buddha's teachings on ethical behavior are based on this principle. It is important to note here that, unlike the theistic religions, Buddhism does not propose an agent or arbitrating force that rewards or punishes good and evil actions. Rather, good and evil actions are seen as causes and conditions that unfold according to the natural flow of events. In this regard, Dhamma (in the sense of ethical teachings) and Dhamma (in the sense of natural reality) are connected in that the Buddhist ethical teachings are based on natural reality. Ethical laws follow the natural law of cause and effect: virtuous actions naturally lead to benefit and evil actions naturally lead to harm, because all of these are factors in the stream of causes and conditions.

Given its dynamic view of the world, Buddhism does not put forth absolute rules for ethical behavior. The ethical value of behavior is judged partly by the results it brings and partly by the qualities which lead to it. Virtuous actions are good because they lead to benefit; evil actions are evil because they lead to harm.

There is a belief that any method used to attain a worthy end is justified by the worthiness of that end. This idea is summed up in the expression "the end justifies the means." Communist revolutionaries, for instance, believed that since the objective is to create an ideal society in which all people are treated fairly, then destroying anybody and anything which stands in the way of that ideal society is justified. The end (the ideal society) justifies the means (hatred and bloodshed).

The idea that "the end justifies the means" is a good example of a human belief which simply does not accord with natural truth. This concept is a human invention, an expedient rationalization which contradicts natural law and "the way things are." Beliefs are not evil in themselves, but when they are in contradiction with reality, they are bound to cause problems. Throughout the ages, people with extreme political and religious ideologies have committed the most brutal acts under the slogan "the end justifies the means." No matter how noble their cause, they ended up destroying that which they were trying to create, which is some kind of happiness or social order.

To learn from history, we must analyze all the causes and conditions that contributed to the unfolding of past events. This includes the qualities of mind of the participants. A thorough analysis of the history of a violent revolution, for example, must consider not only the economic and social climate of the society, but also the emotional and intellectual makeup of the revolutionaries themselves and question the rational validity of the intellectual ideals and methods used, because all of these factors have a bearing on the outcome.

With this kind of analysis, it becomes obvious that, by the natural laws of cause and effect, it is impossible to create an ideal society out of anything less than ideal means—and certainly not bloodshed and hatred. Buddhism would say that it is not the end which justifies the means, but rather the means which *condition* the end. Thus, the result of slaughter and hatred is further violence and instability. This can be witnessed in police states and governments produced by violent revolution—there is always an aftermath of tension, the results of *kamma*, which often proves to be intolerable and social collapse soon follows. Thus the means (bloodshed and aggression) condition the end (tension and instability).

Yet while ethics are subject to these natural laws, when we have to make personal ethical choices right and wrong are not always so obvious. Indeed, the question of ethics is always a highly subjective matter. Throughout our lives, we continually face—and must answer for ourselves—questions of right and wrong. Our every choice, our every intention, holds some ethical judgement.

The Buddhist teachings on matters relating to good and evil serve as guides to help us with these subjective moral choices. But while they are subjective, we should not forget that our ethical choices inevitably play themselves out in the world according to the objective principle of causes and conditions. Our ethics—and the behavior that naturally flows from our ethics—contribute to the causes and conditions that determine who we are, the kind of society we live in and the condition of our environment.

One of the most profound lessons of the Buddha's teachings is the truth that internal, subjective values are directly linked to the dynamic of external objective reality. This subtle realization is at the heart of all ethical questions. Unfortunately, most people are only vaguely aware of how their internal values condition external reality. It is easy to observe the laws of cause and effect in the physical world: ripe apples fall from trees and water runs down hill. But because people tend to think of themselves as individuals separate from the universe, they fail to see how the same laws apply to internal subjective values, such as thoughts and moral attitudes. Since ethics are "subjective," people think they are somehow unconnected to "objective" reality.

According to the Buddhist view, however, ethics forms a bridge between internal and external realities. In accordance with the law of causes and conditions, ethics act as "subjective" causes for "objective" conditions. This should be obvious when we consider that, in essence, ethical questions always ask, "Do my thoughts, words and deeds help or harm myself and those around me?" In practice, we rely on ethics to regulate the unwholesome desires of our subjective reality: anger, greed, hatred. The quality of our thoughts, though internal, constantly conditions the way we speak and act. Though subjective, our ethics determine the kind of impact our life makes on the external, objective world.

How Ethics Condition Economics

To be sure, the distinction between economics and ethics is easily discernible. We can look at any economic situation either from an entirely economic perspective, or from an entirely ethical one. For example, you are reading this book. From an ethical perspective, your reading is a good action, you are motivated by a desire for knowledge. This is an ethical judgement. From the economic perspective, on the other hand, this book may seem to be a waste of resources with no clear benefit. The same situation can be seen in different ways.

However, the two perspectives are interconnected and do influence each other. While modern economic thinking rejects any subjective values like ethics, the influence of ethics in economic matters is all too obvious. If a community is unsafe—if there are thieves, the threat of violence, and the roads are unsafe to travel—then it is obvious that businesses will not invest there, tourists will not want to go there, and the economy will suffer. On the other hand, if the citizens are law-abiding, well-disciplined and conscientiously help to keep their community safe and clean, businesses will have a much better chance of success and the municipal authorities will not have to spend so much on civic maintenance and security.

Unethical business practices have direct economic consequences. If businesses attempt to fatten their profits by using substandard ingredients in foodstuffs, such as by using cloth-dye as a coloring in children's sweets, substituting chemicals for orange juice, or putting boric acid in meatballs (all of which have occurred in Thailand in recent years), consumers' health is endangered. The people made ill by these practices have to pay medical costs and the government has to spend money on police investigations and prosecution of the offenders. Furthermore, the people whose health has suffered work less efficiently, causing a decline in productivity. In international trade, those who pass off shoddy goods as quality merchandise risk losing the trust of their customers and foreign markets—as well as the foreign currency obtained through those markets.

Ethical qualities also influence industrial output. If workers enjoy their work and are industrious, productivity will be high. On the other hand, if they are dishonest, disgruntled or lazy, this will have a negative effect on the quality of production and the amount of productivity.

When it comes to consumption, consumers in a society with vain and fickle values will prefer flashy and ostentatious products to high quality products which are not so flashy. In a more practically-minded society, where the social values do not tend toward showiness and extravagance, consumers will choose goods on the basis of their reliability. Obviously, the goods consumed in these two different societies will lead to different social and economic results.

Advertising stimulates economic activity, but often at an ethically unacceptable price. Advertising is bound up with popular values: advertisers must draw on common aspirations, prejudices and desires in order to produce advertisements that are appealing. Employing social psychology, advertising manipulates popular values for economic ends, and because of its repercussions on the popular mind, it has considerable ethical significance. The volume of advertising may cause an increase in materialism, and unskillful images or messages may harm public morality. The vast majority of ads imbue the public with a predilection for selfish indulgence; they condition us into being perfect consumers who have no higher purpose in life than to consume the products of modern industry. In the process, we are transformed into 'hungry ghosts,' striving to feed an everlasting craving, and society becomes a seething mass of conflicting interests.

Moreover, advertising adds to the price of the product itself. Thus people tend to buy unnecessary things at prices that are unnecessarily expensive. There is much wastage and extravagance. Things are used for a short while and then replaced, even though they are still in good condition. Advertising also caters to peoples' tendency to flaunt their possessions as a way of gaining social status. When snob-appeal is the main criterion, people buy unnecessarily expensive products without considering the quality. In extreme cases, people are so driven by the need to appear stylish that they cannot wait to save the money for the latest gadget or fashion—they simply use their credit cards. Spending in excess of earnings can become a vicious cycle. A newer model or fashion is advertised and people plunge themselves deeper and deeper into debt trying to keep up. In this way, unethical advertising can lead people to financial ruin. It is ironic that, with the vast amount of 'information technology' available, most of it is used to generate 'misinformation' or delusion.

On the political plane, decisions have to be made regarding policy on advertising—should there be any control, and if so, of what kind? How is one to achieve the proper balance between moral and economic concerns? Education is also involved. Ways may have to be found to teach people to be aware of how advertising works, to reflect on it, and to consider how much of it is to be believed. Good education should seek to make people more intelligent in making decisions about buying goods. The question of advertising demonstrates how activities prevalent in society may have to be considered from many perspectives, all of which are interrelated.

Taking a wider perspective, it can be seen that the free market system itself is ultimately based on a minimum of ethics. The freedom of the free market system may be lost through businesses using unscrupulous means of competition; the creation of a monopoly through influence is one common example, the use of thugs to assassinate a competitor a more unorthodox one. The violent elimination of rivals heralds the end of the free market system, although it is a method scarcely mentioned in the economics textbooks.

To be ethically sound, economic activity must take place in a way that is not harmful to the individual, society or the natural environment. In other words, economic activity should not cause problems for oneself, agitation in society or degeneration of the ecosystem, but rather enhance well-being in these three spheres. If ethical values were factored into economic analysis, a cheap but nourishing meal would certainly be accorded more value than a bottle of whiskey.

Thus, an economics inspired by Buddhism would strive to see and accept the truth of all things. It would cast a wider, more comprehensive eye on the question of ethics. Once ethics has been accepted as a legitimate subject for consideration, ethical questions then become factors to be studied within the whole causal process. But if no account is taken of ethical considerations, economics will be incapable of developing any understanding of the whole causal process, of which ethics forms an integral part.

Modern economics has been said to be the most scientific of all the social sciences. Indeed, priding themselves on their scientific methodology, economists take only measurable quantities into consideration. Some even assert that economics is purely a science of numbers, a matter of mathematical equations. In its efforts to be scientific, economics ignores all non-quantifiable, abstract values.

But by considering economic activity in isolation from other forms of human activity, modern economists have fallen into the narrow specialization characteristic of the industrial age. In the manner of specialists, economists try to eliminate all noneconomic factors from their considerations of human activity and concentrate on a single perspective, that of their own discipline.

In recent years, critics of economics, even a number of economists themselves, have challenged this "objective" position and asserted that economics is the most value-dependent of all the social sciences. It may be asked how it is possible for economics to be free of values when, in fact, it is rooted in the human mind. The economic process begins with want, continues with choice, and ends with satisfaction, all of which are functions of mind. Abstract values are thus the beginning, the middle and the end of economics, and so it is impossible for economics to be value-free. Yet as it stands, many economists avoid any consideration of values, ethics, or mental qualities, despite the fact that these will always have a bearing on economic concerns. Economists' lack of ethical training and their ignorance of the workings of mental values and human desire is a major shortcoming which will prevent them from solving the problems it is their task to solve. If the world is to be saved from the ravages of overconsumption and overproduction, economists must come to an understanding of the importance of ethics to their field. Just as they might study ecology, they should also study ethics and the nature of human desire, and understand them thoroughly. Here is one area in which Buddhism can be of great help.

Chapter Two

The Buddhist View of Human Nature

According to the teachings of Buddhism, human beings are born in a state of ignorance. Ignorance is lack of knowledge, and it is this lack of knowledge that causes problems in life. That human beings are born with ignorance, and are troubled by it right from birth, is obvious when observing the plight of a newborn baby, who cannot talk, look for food or even feed itself.

Ignorance is a real limitation in life; it is a burden, a problem. In Buddhism this burden is called *dukkha* or suffering. Because human beings are born with ignorance, they do not really know how to conduct their lives. Without the guidance of knowledge or wisdom, they simply follow their desires, struggling at the directives of craving to stay alive in a hostile world. In Buddhism this blind craving is called *taṇhā*.

Taṇhā means craving, ambition, restlessness, or thirst. It arises dependent on feeling and is rooted in ignorance. Whenever a sensation of any kind is experienced, be it pleasing or displeasing—such as a beautiful or ugly sight, or a pleasant or unpleasant sound—it is followed by a feeling, either pleasant, unpleasant or neutral. Taṇhā arises in correspondence with the feeling: if the feeling is pleasant, there will be a desire to hold onto it; if the feeling is unpleasant, there will be a desire to escape from or destroy it; if the feeling is neutral, there will be a subtle kind of attachment to it. These reactions are automatic, they do not require any conscious intention or any special knowledge or understanding. (On the contrary, if some reflection does interrupt the process at any time, taṇhā may be intercepted, and the process rechannelled into a new form.)

Because taṇhā so closely follows feeling, it tends to seek out objects which will provide pleasant feelings, which are basically the six kinds of pleasant sense objects: sights, sounds, smells, tastes, bodily feelings and mental objects. The most prominent of these are the first five, known as the five sense pleasures. The six sense objects, and particularly the five sense pleasures, are the objects that taṇhā seeks out and fixes onto. In this context, our definition of taṇhā might be expanded on thus: taṇhā is the craving for sense objects which provide pleasant feeling, or craving for sense pleasures. In brief, taṇhā could be called wanting to have or wanting to obtain.

The way taṇhā works can been seen in the basic need for food. The biological purpose of eating is to nourish the body, to provide it with strength and well-being. Supplanted over this biological need is the desire for enjoyment, for delicious tastes. This is taṇhā. At times, the desire of taṇhā may be at odds with well-being, and may even be detrimental to the quality of life. If we are overwhelmed by taṇhā when we eat, rather than eating for the purpose of nourishing the body and providing it with well-being, we eat for the experience of the pleasant taste. This kind of eating knows no end and can lead to problems in both body and mind. The food may be delicious, but we may end up suffering from indigestion or obesity. On a wider scale, the social costs of overconsumption, such as depletion of natural resources and costs incurred by health care, not to mention crime, corruption and wars, are enormous.

Modern economics and Buddhism both agree that mankind has unlimited wants. As the Buddha said, "There is no river like craving."[1] Rivers can sometimes fill their banks, but the wants of human beings can never be filled. Even if money were to fall from the skies like rain, man's sensual desires would not be satisfied.[2] The Buddha also said that even if one could magically transform one single mountain into two mountains of solid gold it would still not provide complete and lasting satisfaction to one person.[3] There are numerous teachings in the Buddhist tradition describing the unlimited nature of human want. Here I would like to relate a story that appears in the Jātaka Tales.[4]

In the far and ancient past there lived a king called Mandhātu. He was a very powerful ruler, an emperor who is known in legend for having lived a very long life. Mandhātu had all the classic requisites of an emperor; he was an exceptional human being who had everything that anyone could wish for: he was a prince for 84,000 years, then the heir apparent for 84,000 years, and then emperor for 84,000 years.

One day, after having been emperor for 84,000 years, King Mandhātu started to show signs of boredom. The great wealth that he possessed was no longer enough to satisfy him. The King's courtiers saw that something was wrong and asked what was ailing His Majesty. He replied, "The wealth and pleasure I enjoy here is trifling. Tell me, is there anywhere superior to this?" "Heaven, Your Majesty," the courtiers replied. Now, one of the King's treasures was the *cakkaratana*, a magic wheel that could transport him anywhere he wished to go. So King Mandhātu used it to take him to the Heaven of the Four Great Kings. The Four Great Kings came out to welcome him in person, and on learning of his desire, invited him to take over the whole of their heavenly realm.

King Mandhātu ruled over the Heaven of the Four Great Kings for a very long time, until one day he began to feel bored again. It was no longer enough, the pleasure that could be derived from the wealth and delights of that realm could satisfy him no more. He conferred with his attendants and was informed of the superior enjoyments of the Tāvatiṁsa Heaven realm. So King Mandhātu picked up his magic wheel and ascended to the Tāvatiṁsa Heaven, where he was greeted by its ruler, Lord Indra, who promptly made him a gift of half of his kingdom.

King Mandhātu ruled over the Tāvatiṁsa Heaven with Lord Indra for another very long time, until Lord Indra came to the end of the merit that had sustained him in his high station, and was replaced by a new Lord Indra. The new Lord Indra ruled on until he too reached the end of his life-span. In all, thirty-six Lord Indras came and went, while King Mandhātu carried on enjoying the pleasures of his position.

Then, finally, he began to feel dissatisfied—half of heaven was not enough, he wanted to rule over all of it. So King Mandhātu began to plot to kill Lord Indra and depose him. But it is impossible for a human being to kill Lord Indra, because humans cannot kill heavenly beings, and so his wish went unfulfilled. King Mandhātu's inability to satisfy this craving began to rot the very root of his being, and caused the aging process to begin.

Suddenly he fell out of Tāvatiṁsa Heaven, down to earth, where he landed in an orchard with a resounding thump. When the workers in the orchard saw that a great king had arrived, some set off to inform the Palace, and others improvised a makeshift throne for him to sit on. By now King Mandhātu was on the verge of death. The Royal Family came out to see and asked if he had any last words. King Mandhātu proclaimed his greatness. He told them of the great power and wealth he had possessed on earth and in heaven, but then finally admitted that his desires remained unfulfilled.

There the story of King Mandhātu ends. It shows how Buddhism shares with economics the view that the wants of humanity are endless.

From Conflict to Harmony

In the struggle to feed their blind and endless desires, people do not clearly perceive what is of true benefit and what is harmful in life. They do not know what leads to true well-being and what leads away from it. With minds blinded by ignorance, people can only strive to feed their desires. In this striving they sometimes create that which is of benefit, and sometimes destroy it. If they do create some well-being, it is usually only incidental to their main objective, but in most cases the things obtained through taṇhā harm the quality of life.

As they struggle against each other and the world around them to fulfill their selfish desires, human beings live in conflict with themselves, with their societies and with the natural environment. There is a conflict of interests; a life guided by ignorance is full of conflict and disharmony.

If this were all there is to human nature, and all that needed to be taken into consideration in economic matters, then we human beings would not be much different from the animals, and perhaps even worse because of our special talent for pursuing activities which are detrimental to well-being. Fortunately, there is more to human nature than this. Buddhism states that human beings are naturally endowed with a special aptitude for development. While Buddhism accepts the fact that it is natural for people to have cravings for things, it also recognizes the human desire for quality of life or well-being, the desire for self improvement and goodness. Problems arise when life is lived from ignorance and at the direction of craving. Problems can be solved by acquiring knowledge. Human development thus hinges on the development of knowledge. In Buddhism we call this kind of knowledge *paññā*, wisdom.

When ignorance is replaced with wisdom, it is possible to distinguish between what is of true benefit and what is not. With wisdom, desires will naturally be for that which is truly beneficial. In Buddhism, this desire for true well-being is called *dhamma-*

chanda (desire for that which is right), *kusalachanda* (desire for that which is skillful), or in short, *chanda*.

The objective of chanda is *dhamma* or *kusaladhamma*, truth and goodness. Truth and goodness must be obtained through effort, and so chanda leads to action, as opposed to taṇhā, which leads to seeking. Chanda arises from intelligent reflection (*yoniso-manasikāra*), as opposed to taṇhā, which is part of the habitual stream of ignorant reactions.

To summarize this:

1. *Taṇhā* is directed toward feeling; it leads to seeking of objects which pander to self interests and is supported and nourished by ignorance.

2. *Chanda* is directed toward benefit, it leads to effort and action, and is founded on intelligent reflection.

As wisdom is developed, chanda becomes more dominant, while the blind craving of taṇhā loses its strength. By training and developing ourselves, we live less and less at the directives of ignorance and taṇhā and more and more under the guidance of wisdom and chanda This leads to a more skillful life, and a much better and more fruitful relationship with the things around us.

With wisdom and chanda we no longer see life as a conflict of interests. Instead, we strive to harmonize our own interests with those of society and nature. The conflict of interests becomes a harmony of interests. This is because we understand that, in the end, a truly beneficial life is only possible when the individual, society and the environment serve each other. If there is conflict between any of these spheres, the result will be problems for all.

Ethics and the Two Kinds of Desire

As we have seen, Buddhism recognizes two different kinds of wanting: (1) taṇhā, the desire for pleasure objects; and (2) chanda, the desire for well-being. Taṇhā is based on ignorance, while chanda is based on wisdom and is thus part of the process of solving problems.

Taṇhā and chanda both lead to satisfaction, but of different kinds. Using the example of eating, people who are driven by taṇhā will seek to satisfy the blind craving for sensual pleasure which, in this case, is the desire for pleasant taste. Here, satisfaction results from experiencing the flavor of the food. But when guided by chanda, desires are directed to realizing well-being. We are not compelled to overeat or to eat the kinds of foods that will make us sick simply because they taste good. Instead, we eat to satisfy hunger and nourish the body. Here satisfaction results from the assurance of well-being provided by the act of eating. We enjoy our food, but not in such a way that leads to remorse.

Chanda leads to effort and action based on intelligence and clear thinking. By contrast, taṇhā leads to blind seeking based on ignorance. Both of these internal desires motivate behavior, but with very different ethical consequences. In Buddhism the ethical value of behavior can be judged by whether it is motivated (overtly) by taṇhā or chanda and (on a deeper level) by ignorance or wisdom. When it comes to judging the ethical value of economic behavior, we must determine what kind of mental state is motivating it. When greed (taṇhā) is driving economic decisions, behavior tends to be morally unskillful, but when desire for well-being (chanda) is guiding them, economic behavior will be morally skillful. By judging economic behavior in this way, we see how mental states, moral behavior and economic activity are linked in the cause and effect stream.

From the Buddhist point of view, economic activity should be a means to a good and noble life. Production, consumption and other economic activities are not ends in themselves; they are means, and the end to which they must lead is the development of well-being within the individual, within society and within the environment.

Contrary to the misconception that Buddhism is only for renunciants, Buddhists recognize that acquiring wealth is one of life's fundamental activities, and the Buddha gave many teachings on the proper way to acquire wealth. But he always stressed that the purpose of wealth is to facilitate the development of highest human potential. In Buddhism there are said to be three goals in life: the initial, medium, and ultimate goals. The initial goal is reasonable material comfort and economic security. Material security, however, is only a foundation for the two higher, more abstract goals—mental well-being and inner freedom.

The major part of our lives is taken up with economic activities. If economics is to have any real part to play in the resolution of human problems, then all economic activities—production, consumption, work and spending—must contribute to well-being and help realize the potential for a good and noble life. It is something that we are capable of doing. The essence of Buddhist economics lies here, in ensuring that economic activity enhances the quality of our lives.

Ethical Considerations in Economic Activity

A fundamental principle of modern economics states that people will only agree to part with something when they can replace it with something that affords them equal or more satisfaction. But this principle only considers the satisfaction that comes from owning material goods. Sometimes we can experience a sense of satisfaction by parting with something without getting anything tangible in return, as when parents give their children gifts: because of the love they feel for their children, they feel a more rewarding sense of satisfaction than if they had received something in return. If human beings could expand their love to all other people, rather than confining it to their own families, then they might be able to part with things without receiving anything in return, and experience more satisfaction in doing so. This satisfaction comes not from a desire to obtain things to make ourselves happy (taṇhā), but from a desire for the well-being of others (chanda).*

---

* *Chanda*, when directed toward other beings, is called *mettā*, goodwill, the desire for others' welfare.

Another economic principle states that the value of goods is determined by demand. This principle is classically illustrated by the story of two men shipwrecked on a desert island: one has a sack of rice and the other a hundred gold necklaces. Ordinarily, a single gold necklace would be enough, more than enough, to buy a whole sack of rice. But now the two men find themselves stranded on an island with no means of escape and no guarantee of rescue. The value of the goods changes. Now the person with the rice might demand all one hundred gold necklaces for a mere portion of the rice, or he might refuse to make the exchange at all.

However the question of ethics does not come into this discussion. Economists may assert that economics only concerns itself with demand, not its ethical quality, but in fact ethical considerations do affect demand. In the example of the two shipwrecked men, there are other possibilities besides trade. The man with the gold necklaces might steal some of the rice while the owner is not watching, or he might just kill him in order to get the whole sack. On the other hand, the two men might become friends and help each other out, sharing the rice until it's all gone, so that there is no need for any buying or selling at all.

In real life, it could happen in any of these ways. Factors such as personal morality or emotions such as greed and fear can and do affect economic outcome. A demand that does not stop at violence or theft will have different results from one that recognizes moral restraints.

One way to evaluate the ethical quality of economic activity is to look at the effects it has on three levels: on the individual consumer, on society and on the environment. Let us return to the example of the bottle of whiskey and the Chinese dinner. It is obvious that, though their market prices may be the same, their economic costs are not equal. The bottle of whiskey may damage the consumer's health, forcing him to spend money on medical treatment. The distillery which produced the whiskey may have released foul-smelling fumes into the air. This pollution has economic repercussions, forcing the government to spend resources on cleaning the environment. Moreover, one who drinks and suffers from a hangover on the job will work less efficiently, or he might get drunk and crash his car, incurring more economic costs. Then there are detrimental social effects: drinking can contribute to crime, which has very high costs for society.

Although ethical questions, they all have economic ramifications. They imply the necessity of looking at economic costs on a much wider scale than at present—not just in terms of market prices. There is now a trend towards including environmental costs in economic calculations. Some economists even include them in the cost of a finished product. But this is not enough. In the case of the bottle of whiskey, apart from the environmental costs, there are also the social, moral, and health costs—inefficient production, auto accidents, liver disease, crime—all of which have economic implications.*

A second way to evaluate the ethical quality of economic activity is to determine which kind of desire is at its root. The most unethical economic activities are those that feed taṇhā while undermining well-being. Trade in tobacco, drugs, and prostitution are examples of detrimental economic activities geared solely toward satisfying a craving for pleasure.

The more people are driven by taṇhā the more they destroy their true well-being. This principle applies not only to the obvious vices, but to all economic activities. Thus, in decisions dealing with consumption, production, and the use of technology, we must learn how to distinguish between the two kinds of desire and make our choices wisely.

* In light of the above, the recent acceptance of environmental costs (because of pressure resulting from the threat of imminent environmental havoc) in economic activity by the economic mainstream, while still ignoring social and ethical costs (because the threat is not yet extreme enough to demand their attention), which are equally as objective, is indeed unusual—a good example of subjectivity in economic thinking.

Chapter Three

Buddhist Perspectives on Economic Concepts

The basic model of economic activity is often represented in economic textbooks thus: unlimited wants are controlled by scarcity; scarcity requires choice; choice involves an opportunity cost (i.e., choosing one means foregoing the other); and the final goal is maximum satisfaction.[1] The fundamental concepts occurring in this model—want, choice, consumption and satisfaction—describe the basic activities of our lives from an economic perspective. These concepts are based on certain assumptions about human nature. Unfortunately, the assumptions modern economists make about human nature are somewhat confused.

Buddhism, on the other hand, offers a clear and consistent picture of human nature: a view which encompasses the role of ethics and the twofold nature of human desire. Let us now take a look at some economic concepts in the light of Buddhist thinking.

Value

In the previous chapter, we discussed the two kinds of desire, *chanda* and *taṇhā*. Given that there are two kinds of desire, it follows that there are two kinds of value, which we might term true value and artificial value. True value is created by chanda. In other words, a commodity's true value is determined by its ability to meet the need for well-being. Conversely, artificial value is created by taṇhā—it is a commodity's capacity to satisfy the desire for pleasure.

To assess an object's value, we must ask ourselves which kind of desire—taṇhā or chanda—defines it. Fashionable clothes, jewelry, luxury cars and other status-symbols contain a high degree of artificial value because they cater to people's vanity and desire for pleasure. A luxury car may serve the same function as a cheaper car, but it commands a higher price largely because of its artificial value. Many of the pleasures taken for granted in today's consumer society—the games, media thrills and untold forms of junk foods available—are created solely for the purpose of satisfying taṇhā, have no practical purpose at all and are often downright detrimental to well-being. For the most part, advertising promotes this artificial value. Advertisers stimulate desires by projecting pleasurable images onto the products they sell. They induce us to believe, for example, that whoever can afford a luxury car will stand out from the crowd and be a member of high society, or that by drinking a certain brand of soft drink we will have lots of friends and be happy.

The true value of an object is typically overshadowed by its artificial value. Craving and conceit, and the desire for the fashionable and sensually appealing, cloud any reckoning of the true value of things. How many people, for instance, reflect on the true value or reasons for eating food or wearing clothes?

Consumption

The question of consumption is similar to that of value. We must distinguish which kind of desire our consumption is intended to satisfy: is it to answer the need for things of true value, or to indulge in the pleasures afforded by artificial value? Consumption is said to be one of the goals of economic activity. However, economic theory and Buddhism define consumption differently.

Consumption is the alleviation or satisfaction of desire, that much is agreed. Modern economics defines consumption as simply the use of goods and services to satisfy demand. Buddhism, however, distinguishes between two kinds of consumption, which might be termed "right" consumption and "wrong" consumption. Right consumption is the use of goods and services to satisfy the desire for true well-being. It is consumption with a goal and a purpose. Wrong consumption arises from taṇhā; it is the use of goods and services to satisfy the desire for pleasing sensations or ego-gratification.

While the Buddhist perspective is based on a wide view of the stream of causes and effects, the specialized thinking of economics identifies only part of the stream: demand leads to consumption which leads to satisfaction. For most economists that's the end of it, there's no need to know what happens afterwards. In this view, consumption can be of anything whatsoever, so long as it results in satisfaction. There is little consideration of whether or not well-being is adversely affected by that consumption.

Consumption may satisfy sensual desires, but its true purpose is to provide well-being. For example, our body depends on food for nourishment. Consumption of food is thus a requirement for well-being. For most people, however, eating food is also a means to experience pleasure. If in consuming food one receives the experience of a delicious flavor, one is said to have satisfied one's desires. Economists tend to think in this way, holding that the experience of satisfaction is the end result of consumption. But here the crucial question is: What is the true purpose of consuming food: satisfaction of desires or the attainment of well-being?

In the Buddhist view, when consumption enhances true well-being, it is said to be successful. On the other hand, if consumption results merely in feelings of satisfaction, then it fails. At its worst, consumption through taṇhā destroys its true objective, which is to enhance well-being. Heedlessly indulging in desires with no regard to the repercussions often leads to harmful effects and a loss of true well-being. Moreover, the compulsive consumption rampant in consumer societies breeds inherent dissatisfaction. It is a strange thing that economics, the science of human well-being and satisfaction, accepts, and indeed lauds, the kind of consumption that in effect frustrates the realization of its own objectives.

By contrast, right consumption always contributes to well-being and forms a basis for the further development of human potentialities. This is an important point often overlooked by economists. Consumption guided by chanda does much more than just satisfy one's desire; it contributes to well-being and spiritual development. This is also true on a global scale. If all economic activities were guided by chanda, the result would be much more than just a healthy economy and material progress—such activities would contribute to the whole of human development and enable mankind to lead a nobler life and enjoy a more mature kind of happiness.

Moderation

At the very heart of Buddhism is the wisdom of moderation. When the goal of economic activity is seen to be satisfaction of desires, economic activity is open-ended and without clear definition—desires are endless. According to the Buddhist approach, economic activity must be controlled by the qualification that it is directed to the attainment of well-being rather than the "maximum satisfaction" sought after by traditional economic thinking. Well-being as an objective acts as a control on economic activity. No longer are we struggling against each other to satisfy endless desires. Instead, our activities are directed toward the attainment of well-being. If economic activity is directed in this way, its objectives are clear and its activities are controlled. A balance or equilibrium is achieved. There is no excess, no overconsumption or overproduction. In the classical economic model, unlimited desires are controlled by scarcity, but in the Buddhist model they are controlled by an appreciation of moderation and the objective of well-being. The resulting balance will naturally eliminate the harmful effects of uncontrolled economic activity.

Buddhist monks and nuns traditionally reflect on moderation before each meal by reciting this reflection:[2]

> Wisely reflecting, we take alms food, not for the purpose of fun, not for indulgence or the fascination of taste, but simply for the maintenance of the body, for the continuance of existence, for the cessation of painful feeling, for living the higher life. Through this eating, we subdue old painful feelings of hunger and prevent new painful feelings (of overeating) from arising. Thus do we live unhindered, blameless, and in comfort.

The goal of moderation is not restricted to monastics: whenever we use things, be it food, clothing, or even paper and electricity, we can take the time to reflect on their true purpose, rather than using them heedlessly. By reflecting in this way we can avoid heedless consumption and so understand "the right amount," the "middle way."

We also come to see consumption as a means to an end, which is the development of human potential. With human development as our goal, we eat food not simply for the pleasure it affords, but to obtain the physical and mental energy necessary for intellectual and spiritual growth toward a nobler life.

Non-consumption

Lacking a spiritual dimension, modern economic thinking encourages maximum consumption. It praises those who eat the most—three, four or more times a day. If someone were to eat ten times a day, so much the better. By contrast, a Buddhist economics understands that non-consumption can contribute to well-being. Though monks eat only one meal a day, they strive for a kind of well-being that is dependent on little.

On Observance days, some Buddhist laypeople also refrain from eating after midday and, in so doing, contribute to their own well-being. Renunciation of the evening meal allows them to spend time in meditation and reflection on the Buddha's teachings. The body is light and the mind easily calmed when the stomach is not full. Thus Buddhism recognizes that certain demands can be satisfied through non-consumption, a position which traditional economic thinking would find hard to appreciate. Refraining from eating can play a role in satisfying our nonmaterial, spiritual needs.

It's not that getting down to eating one meal a day is the goal, of course. Like consumption, non-consumption is only a means to an end, not an end in itself. If abstinence did not lead to well-being, it would be pointless, just a way of mistreating ourselves. The question is not whether to consume or not to consume, but whether or not our choices lead to self-development.

Overconsumption

Today's society encourages overconsumption. In their endless struggle to find satisfaction through consuming, a great many people damage their own health and harm others. Drinking alcohol, for instance, satisfies a desire, but is a cause of ill-health, unhappy families and fatal accidents. People who eat for taste often overeat and make themselves ill. Others give no thought at all to food values and waste money on junk foods. Some people even become deficient in certain vitamins and minerals despite eating large meals every day. (Incredibly, cases of malnutrition have been reported.) Apart from doing themselves no good, their overeating deprives others of food.

So we cannot say that a thing has value simply because it provides pleasure and satisfaction. If satisfaction is sought in things that do not enrich the quality of life, the result often becomes the destruction of true welfare, leading to delusion and intoxication, loss of health and well-being.

A classic economic principle states that the essential value of goods lies in their ability to bring satisfaction to the consumer. Here we may point to the examples given above where heavy consumption and strong satisfaction have both positive and negative results. The Buddhist perspective is that the benefit of goods and services lies in their ability to provide the consumer with a sense of satisfaction at having enhanced the quality of his or her life. This extra clause is essential. All definitions, whether of goods, services, or personal and social wealth, must be modified in this way.

Contentment

While not technically an economic concern, I would like to add a few comments on the subject of contentment. Contentment is a virtue that has often been misunderstood and, as it relates to consumption and satisfaction, it seems to merit some discussion.

The tacit objective of economics is a dynamic economy where every demand and desire is supplied and constantly renewed in a never-ending and ever-growing cycle. The entire mechanism is fuelled by taṇhā. From the Buddhist perspective, this tireless search to satisfy desires is itself a kind of suffering. Buddhism proposes the cessation of this kind of desire, or contentment, as a more skillful objective.

Traditional economists would probably counter that without desire, the whole economy would grind to a halt. However, this is based on a misunderstanding of the nature of contentment. People misunderstand contentment because they fail to distinguish between the two different kinds of desire, taṇhā and chanda. We lump them together, and in proposing contentment, dismiss them both. A contented person comes to be seen as one who wants nothing at all. Here lies our mistake.

Obviously, people who are content will have fewer wants than those who are discontent. However, a correct definition of contentment must be qualified by the stipulation that it implies only the absence of artificial want, that is taṇhā; chanda, the desire for true well-being, remains. In other words, the path to true contentment involves reducing the artificial desire for sense-pleasure, while actively encouraging and supporting the desire for quality of life.

These two processes—reducing taṇhā and encouraging chanda—are mutually supportive. When we are easily satisfied in material things, we save time and energy that might otherwise be wasted on seeking objects of taṇhā. The time and energy we save can, in turn, be applied to the development of well-being, which is the objective of chanda. When it comes to developing skillful conditions, however, contentment is not a beneficial quality. Skillful conditions must be realized through effort. Too much contentment with regards to chanda easily turns into complacency and apathy. In this connection, the Buddha pointed out that his own attainment of enlightenment was largely a result of two qualities: unremitting effort, and lack of contentment with skillful conditions.[3]

Work

Buddhist and conventional economics also have different understandings of the role of work. Modern Western economic theory is based on the view that work is something that we are compelled to do in order to obtain money for consumption. It is during the time when we are not working, or "leisure time," that we may experience happiness and satisfaction. Work and satisfaction are considered to be separate and generally opposing principles.

Buddhism, however, recognizes that work can either be satisfying or not satisfying, depending on which of the two kinds of desire is motivating it. When work stems from the desire for true well-being, there is satisfaction in the direct and immediate results of the work itself. By contrast, when work is done out of desire for pleasure-objects, then the direct results of the work itself are not so important. With this attitude, work is simply an unavoidable necessity to obtain the desired object. The difference between these two attitudes determines whether or not work will directly contribute to well-being. In the first case, work is a potentially satisfying activity, and in the second, it is a necessary chore.

As an example of these two different attitudes, let us imagine two research workers. They are both investigating natural means of pest control for agricultural use. The first researcher, Mr. Smith, desires the direct fruits of his research—knowledge and its practical application—and takes pride in his work. The discoveries and advances he makes afford him a sense of satisfaction.

The second, Mr. Jones, only works for money and promotions. Knowledge and its application, the direct results of his work, are not really what he desires; they are merely the means through which he can ultimately obtain money and position. Mr. Jones doesn't enjoy his work, he does it because he feels he has to.

Work performed in order to meet the desire for well-being can provide inherent satisfaction, because it is appreciated for its own sake. Achievement and progress in the work lead to a growing sense of satisfaction at every stage of the work's development. In Buddhist terminology, this is called working with chanda. Conversely, working out of desire for pleasure is called working with taṇhā. Those working with taṇhā are motivated by the desire to consume. But since it is impossible to consume and work at the same time, the work itself affords little enjoyment or satisfaction. It should also be pointed out that work in this case postpones the attainment of satisfaction, and as such will be seen as an impediment to it. When work is seen as an impediment to consumption it can become intolerable. In developing countries this is readily seen in the extent of hire-purchase debt and corruption, where consumers cannot tolerate the delay between working and consuming the objects of their desires.

In modern industrial economies, many jobs preclude satisfaction, or make it very difficult, by their very nature. Factory jobs can be dull, undemanding, pointless, even dangerous to health. They breed boredom, frustration, and depression, all of which have negative effects on productivity. However, even in menial or insignificant tasks, there is a difference between working with taṇhā and working with chanda. Even in the most monotonous of tasks, where one may have difficulty generating a sense of pride in the object of one's labors, a desire to perform the task well, or a sense of pride in one's own endeavors, may help to alleviate the monotony, and even contribute something of a sense of achievement to the work: even though the work may be monotonous, one feels that at least one is developing good qualities like endurance and is able to derive a certain enthusiasm for the work.

As we have seen, the fulfillment of taṇhā lies with seeking and obtaining objects which provide pleasant feelings. While this seeking may involve action, the objective of taṇhā is not directly related in a causal way to the action undertaken. Let's look at two different tasks and examine the cause and effect relationships involved: (1) Mr. Smith sweeps the street, and is paid $500 a month; (2) If Little Suzie finishes the book she is reading, Daddy will take her to the movies.

It may seem at first glance that sweeping the street is the cause for Mr. Smith receiving his wage; that is, sweeping the street is the cause, and money is the result. But in fact, this is a mistaken conclusion. Correctly speaking, one would say: the action of sweeping the street is the cause for the street being cleaned; the cleanness of the street is a stipulation for Mr. Smith receiving his wage, based on an agreement between employer and employee.

All actions have results that arise as a natural consequence. The natural result of sweeping the street is a clean street. In the contract between employer and employee, a stipulation is added to this natural result, so that sweeping the street also brings about a payment of money. This is a man-made, or artificial, law. However, money is not the natural result of sweeping the street: some people may sweep a street and get no money for it, while many other people receive wages without having to sweep streets. Money is a socially contrived or artificial condition. Many contemporary social problems result from confusion between the natural results of actions and the human stipulations added to them. People begin to think that a payment of money really is the natural result of sweeping a street, or, to use another example, that a good wage, rather than medical knowledge, is the natural result of studying medicine.

As for Little Suzie, it may seem that completing the book is the cause, and going to the movies with Dad is the result. But in fact finishing the book is simply a stipulation on which going to the movies is based. The true result of reading the book is obtaining knowledge.

Expanding on these examples, if Mr. Smith's work is directed solely by taṇhā, all he wants is his $500, not the cleanness of the street. In fact, he doesn't want to sweep the street at all, but, since it is a condition for receiving his wage, he must. As for Little Suzie, if her true desire is to go to the movies (not to read the book), then reading will afford no satisfaction in itself; she only reads because it is a condition for going to the movies.

When people work solely out of taṇhā, their true desire is for consumption, not action. Their actions—in this case, sweeping and reading—are seen as means of obtaining the objects of desire—the salary and a trip to the movies. When they work with chanda, on the other hand, Mr. Smith takes pride in (i.e., desires) the cleanness of the street and little Suzie wants the knowledge contained in the book. With chanda, their desire is for action and the true results of that action. Cleanness is the natural result of sweeping the street and knowledge is the natural result of reading the book. When the action is completed, the result naturally and simultaneously arises. When Mr. Smith sweeps the street, a clean street ensues, and it ensues whenever he sweeps. When Little

Suzie reads a book, knowledge arises, and it arises whenever she reads the book. With chanda, work is intrinsically satisfying because it is itself the achievement of the desired result.

Thus, the objective of chanda is action and the good result which arises from it. When their actions are motivated by chanda, Mr. Smith applies himself to sweeping the street irrespective of his monthly wage, and little Suzie will read her book even without Daddy having to promise to take her to the movies. (In reality, of course, most people do work for the wages, which are a necessity, but we also have the choice to take pride in our work and strive to do it well, which is chanda, or to do it perfunctorily simply for the wage. Thus, in real life situations, most people are motivated by varying degrees of both taṇhā and chanda.)

As we have seen, actions motivated by chanda and actions motivated by taṇhā give rise to very different results, both objectively and ethically. When we are motivated by taṇhā and are working simply to attain an unrelated object or means of consumption, we may be tempted to attain the object of desire through other means which involve less effort. If we can obtain the objective without having to do any work at all, even better. If it is absolutely necessary to work for the objective, however, we will only do so reluctantly and perfunctorily.

The extreme result of this is criminal activity. If Mr. Smith wants money but has no desire (chanda) to work, he may find working for the money intolerable and so resort to theft. If Little Suzie wants to go the movies, but can't stand reading the book, she may steal money from her mother and go to the movies herself.

With only taṇhā to get their salary but no chanda to do their work, people will only go about the motions of performing their duties, doing just enough to get by. The result is apathy, laziness and poor workmanship. Mr. Smith simply goes through the motions of sweeping the street day by day until pay day arrives, and Little Suzie reads the book simply to let Daddy see that she has finished it, but doesn't take in anything she has read, or she may cheat, saying she has read the book when in fact she hasn't.

When sloppiness and dishonesty of this type arise within the work place, secondary checks must be established to monitor the work. These measures address the symptoms but not the cause, and only add to the complexity of the situation. For example, it may be necessary to install a supervisor to inspect Mr. Smith's work and check his hours; or Little Suzie's brother may have to look in and check that she really is reading the book. This applies to employers as well as employees: workers' tribunals must be established to prevent greedy or irresponsible employers from exploiting their workers and making them work in inhumane conditions or for unfair wages. When taṇhā is the motivating force, workers and employers are trapped in a game of one-upmanship, with each side trying to get as much for themselves as they can for the least possible expense.

Taṇhā is escalated to a considerable extent by social influences. For instance, when the owners of the means of production are blindly motivated by a desire to get rich for as little outlay as possible, it is very unlikely that the workers will have much chanda. They will be more likely to follow the example of their employers, trying to get as much as they can for as little effort as possible. This tendency can be seen in the modern work place. It seems, moreover, that the more affluent a society becomes, the more this tendency is produced—the more we have, the more we want. This is a result of the unchecked growth of taṇhā and the lack of any viable alternative. Meanwhile, the values of inner contentment and peace of mind seem to have been all but lost in modern society.

In rare cases, however, we hear of employers and employees who do work together with chanda. This happens when the employer is responsible, capable and considerate, thus commanding the confidence and affection of employees, who in return are harmonious, diligent, and committed to their work. There have even been cases of employers who were so caring with their employees that when their businesses failed and came close to bankruptcy, the employees sympathetically made sacrifices and worked as hard as possible to make the company profitable again. Rather than making demands for compensation, they were willing to take a cut in wages.

Production and Non-production

The word "production" is misleading. We tend to think that through production new things are created, when in fact it is merely changes of state which are effected. One substance or form of energy is converted into another. These conversions entail the creation of a new state by the destruction of an old one. Thus production is always accompanied by destruction. In some cases the destruction is acceptable, in others it is not. Production is only truly justified when the value of the thing produced outweighs the value of that which is destroyed. In some cases it may be better to refrain from production. This is invariably true for those industries whose products are for the purpose of destruction. In weapons factories, for example, non-production is always the better choice. In industries where production entails the destruction of natural resources and environmental degradation, non-production is sometimes the better choice. To choose, we must distinguish between production with positive results and production with negative results; production that enhances well-being and that which destroys it.

In this light, non-production can be a useful economic activity. A person who produces very little in materialistic terms may, at the same time, consume much less of the world's resources and lead a life that is beneficial to the world around him. Such a person is of more value than one who diligently consumes large amounts of the world's resources while manufacturing goods that are harmful to society. But modern economics could never make such a distinction; it would praise a person who produces and consumes (that is, destroys) vast amounts more than one who produces and consumes (destroys) little.

In the economics of the industrial era the term production has been given a very narrow meaning. It is taken to relate only to those things that can be bought and sold—a bull fight, where people pay money to see bulls killed, is seen as contributing to the economy, while a child helping an elderly person across the street is not; a professional comedian telling jokes on stage, relaxing his audience and giving them a good time, is taken to be economically productive because money changes hands, while an office worker with a very cheerful disposition is not considered to have produced anything by his cheerfulness toward those around him. Nor is there any accounting of the economic costs of aggressive action and speech that continually create tension in the work place, so that those affected have to find some way to alleviate it with amusements, such as going to see a comedian.

Competition and Cooperation

Modern economics is based on the assumption that it is human nature to compete. Buddhism, on the other hand, recognizes that human beings are capable of both competition and cooperation.

Competition is natural: when they are striving to satisfy the desire for pleasure—when they are motivated by taṇhā—people will compete fiercely. At such times they want to get as much as possible for themselves and feel no sense of sufficiency or satisfaction. If they can obtain the desired object without having to share it with anyone else, so much the better. Inevitably, competition is intense; this is natural for the mind driven by taṇhā.

This competitive instinct can be redirected to induce cooperation. One might unite the members of a particular group by inciting them to compete with another group. For example, corporate managers sometimes rally their employees to work together to beat their competitors. But this cooperation is based entirely on competition. Buddhism would call this "artificial cooperation."

True cooperation arises with the desire for well-being—with chanda. Human development demands that we understand how taṇhā and chanda motivate us and that we shift our energies from competition towards cooperative efforts to solve the problems facing the world and to realize a nobler goal.

Choice

"Whether a given want is a true need, a fanciful desire, or a bizarre craving is of no matter to economics. Nor is it the business of economics to judge whether such wants should be satisfied,"[4] say the economics texts, but from a Buddhist perspective the choices we make are of utmost importance, and these choices require some qualitative appreciation of the options available. Choice is a function of intention, which is the heart of kamma, one of Buddhism's central teachings. The influence of kamma affects not only economics but all areas of our lives and our social and natural environment. Economic decisions, or choices, which lack ethical reflection are bad kamma—they are bound to bring undesirable results. Good economic decisions are those based on an awareness of the costs on the individual, social and environmental levels, not just in terms of production and consumption. These economic decisions are kamma. Every time an economic decision is made, kamma is made, and the process of fruition is immediately set in motion, for better or for worse, for the individual, for society and the environment. Thus it is important to recognize the qualitative difference between different courses of action and to make our choices wisely.

Life Views

I would now like to take a step back and look at economics from a somewhat wider perspective. We have discussed the various economic activities. We may now ask: what is the purpose of these activities? What are we striving for in all this buying and selling, producing and consuming? Or we may ask an even grander question: What indeed is the purpose of life?

Everybody holds views on these matters, although most of us are unconscious of them. Buddhist teachings stress that these views exert a tremendous influence on our lives. The Pali word for view is *diṭṭhi*. This term covers all kinds of views on many different levels—our personal opinions and beliefs; the ideologies, religious and political views espoused by groups; and the attitudes and world-views held by whole cultures and societies.

Views lead to ramifications far beyond the realm of mental states and intellectual discourse. Like ethics, views are linked to the stream of causes and conditions. They are "subjective" mental formations that inevitably condition events in "objective" reality. On a personal level, one's world-view affects the events of life. On a national level, political views and social mores condition society and the quality of day-to-day life.

The Buddha warned that views are potentially the most dangerous of all mental conditions. Unskillful views can wreak unimaginable damage. The violence of the Crusades, Nazism and Communism, to name just three disastrous fanatical movements, were fuelled by extremely unskillful views. Skillful views, on the other hand, are the most beneficial of mental conditions. As the Buddha said: "Monks, I see no other condition which is so much a cause for the arising of as yet unarisen unskillful conditions, and for the development and fruition of unskillful conditions already arisen, as wrong view ... "[5]

This begs the question: what view of life is behind modern economics? Is it a skillful or an unskillful one? At the risk of oversimplifying, let us say that the goal of modern life is to find happiness. This view is so pervasive in modern societies that it is rarely even recognized, let alone examined or questioned. The very concept of "progress"—social, economic, scientific and political—assumes that society's highest goal is to reach a state where everyone will be happy. The United States Declaration of Independence poetically embodies this ideal by asserting mankind's right to "life, liberty and the pursuit of happiness."

While certainly a good-hearted aspiration, the view that happiness is the goal of life betrays a fundamental confusion about the truth of life. "Happiness" is never more than an ill-defined, elusive quality. Many people equate happiness with sense pleasure and the satisfaction of their desires. For these people, happiness remains a remote condition, something outside themselves, a future prize that must be pursued and captured. But happiness cannot be obtained through seeking, only through bringing about the causes and conditions which lead to it, and these are personal and mental development.

From the Buddhist point of view, people often confuse taṇhā—their restless craving for satisfaction and pleasure—with the pursuit of happiness. This is indeed an unskillful view, because the craving of taṇhā can never be satisfied. If the pursuit of happiness equals the pursuit of the objects of taṇhā, then life itself becomes a misery. To see the consequences of this unfortunate view, one need only witness the depression and angst of the citizens in so many modern cities filled with limitless distractions and pleasure centers. Rather than leading to contentment and well-being, the pursuit of happiness so often leads to restlessness and exhaustion in the individual, strife in society and unsustainable consumption of the environment.

By contrast, the Buddhist view of life is much less idealistic but much more practical. The Buddha said simply, "There is suffering."[6] This was the first of his Four Noble Truths, the central tenets of Buddhism. He went on to describe what suffering is: "Birth is suffering; old age is suffering; sickness is suffering; death is suffering; sorrow, lamentation, pain, grief and despair are suffering; separation from the loved is suffering; getting what you don't want is suffering; not getting what you want is suffering... "

There is little question that these things exist in life and they are all unpleasant, but the tendency of our society is to deny them. Death, in particular, is rarely thought or spoken about as a personal inevitability. Denying these things, however, does not make them go away. This is why the Buddha said that suffering is something that should be recognized. The first Noble Truth is the recognition that all things must pass and that ultimately there is no security to be had within the material world. This is the kind of truth the Buddha urged people to face—the painfully obvious and fundamental facts of life.

The second Noble Truth explains the cause of suffering. The Buddha said that suffering is caused by craving based on ignorance (that is, taṇhā). In other words, the cause of suffering is an internal condition. We may ask, "Does craving cause old age?": it is not craving that causes old age, but rather craving for youth which makes old age a cause of suffering. Old age is inevitable; craving is not. The Buddha said that craving can be eliminated, which brings us to the third Noble Truth, which concerns the cessation of suffering. With the complete and utter abandonment of craving, suffering ceases. But how to do that? In the fourth Noble Truth the Buddha tells how. It is the Noble Eightfold Path for the cessation of suffering, through training of body, speech and mind in accordance with the Buddhist code of Right View, Right Thought, Right Speech, Right Action, Right Livelihood, Right Effort, Right Mindfulness and Right Concentration.

It is fairly obvious from the Four Noble Truths that the Buddhist view of life is very much at odds with the view common to modern societies. Whereas Buddhism says "There is suffering," modern societies say, "There is happiness, and I want it now!" The implications of this simple shift in perception are enormous. A society that views the purpose of life as the pursuit of happiness is one that is recklessly pursuing some future dream. Happiness is seen as something that is inherently lacking and must be found somewhere else. Along with this view comes dissatisfaction, impatience, contention, an inability to deal with suffering, and a lack of attention to the present moment.

On the other hand, with a view of life that appreciates the reality of suffering, we pay more attention to the present moment so that we can recognize problems when they arise. We cooperate with others to solve problems, rather than competing with them to win happiness. Such a view also influences our economic choices. Our production and consumption are geared less toward the pursuit of sense gratification (taṇhā) and more toward relieving suffering (chanda). If this Buddhist view were taken up on a national or global scale, rather than seeking to satisfy every demand, our economies would strive to create a state free of suffering, or a state which is primed for the enjoyment of happiness (just as a healthy body is one which is primed to enjoy happiness).

Only through understanding suffering can we realize the possibility of happiness. Here Buddhism makes a distinction between two kinds of happiness: dependent happiness and independent happiness. Dependent happiness is happiness that requires an external object. It includes any happiness contingent on the material world, including wealth, family, honor and fame. Dependent happiness, being dependent on things that can never be ours in an ultimate sense, is fickle and uncertain.

Independent happiness, on the other hand, is the happiness that arises from within a mind that has been trained and has attained some degree of inner peace. Such a happiness is not dependent on externals and is much more stable than dependent happiness.

Dependent happiness leads to competition and conflict in the struggle to acquire material goods. Any happiness arising from such activity is a contentious kind of happiness. There is, however, a third kind of happiness which, while not as exalted as the truly independent kind, is nevertheless more skillful than the contentious kind. It is a happiness that is more altruistically based, directed toward well-being and motivated by goodwill and compassion. Through personal development, people can appreciate this truer kind of happiness—the desire to bring happiness to others (which in Buddhism we call *mettā*). With this kind of happiness, we can experience gladness at the happiness of others, just as parents feel glad at the happiness of their children. This kind of happiness might be called "harmonious happiness," as distinct from the contentious kind of happiness. It is less dependent on the acquisition of material goods and arises more from giving than receiving. Although such happiness is not truly independent, it is much more skillful than the happiness resulting from selfish acquisition.

The most assured level of happiness is the liberation resulting from enlightenment, which is irreversible. But even to train the mind, through study and meditation practice, to achieve some inner contentment is a powerful antidote to the dissatisfaction of the consumer society. And with the clarity of inner calm comes an insight into one of life's profound ironies: striving for happiness, we create suffering; understanding suffering, we find peace.

Chapter Four

The Role of Wealth in Buddhism

Although Buddhism has been characterized as an ascetic religion, asceticism was in fact experimented with and rejected by the Buddha before he attained enlightenment. As far as Buddhism is concerned, the meaning of the word 'asceticism' is ambiguous and should not be used without qualification.

The term 'poverty' is also misleading. The familiar Buddhist concepts are rather contentment (*santuṭṭhi*) or limited desires (*appicchatā*). Poverty (*dadiddiya*) is in no place praised or encouraged in Buddhism. As the Buddha said, "For householders in this world, poverty is suffering"[1]; "Woeful in the world is poverty and debt."[2]

In fact, the possession of wealth by certain people is often praised and encouraged in the Pali Canon, indicating that wealth is something to be sought after. Among the Buddha's lay disciples, the better known, the most helpful, and the most often praised were in large part wealthy persons, such as Anāthapiṇḍika.

Even for the monks, who are not expected to seek wealth, to be a frequent recipient of offerings was sometimes regarded as a good quality. The monk Sivali, for example, was praised by the Buddha as the foremost of those "who are obtainers of offerings." However, these remarks must be qualified.

The main theme in the Scriptures is that it is not wealth as such that is praised or blamed but the way it is acquired and used. For the monks, as mentioned above, it is not acquisition as such that is blamed, nor poverty that is praised. Blameworthy qualities are greed for gain, stinginess, grasping, attachment to gain and hoarding of wealth. Acquisition is acceptable if it is helpful in the practice of the Noble Path or if it benefits fellow members of the Order.

On the other hand, this does not mean that monks are encouraged to own possessions. As long as it is allowed by the *Vinaya*, or monastic code, gain is justifiable if the possessions belong to the monastic community, but if a monk is rich in personal possessions, it is evidence of his greed and attachment and he cannot be said to conform to Buddhist principles. The right practice for monks is to own nothing except the basic requisites of life. Here the question is not one of being rich or poor, but of having few personal cares, easy mobility, the spirit of contentment and few wishes, and, as the monk's life is dependent for material support on other people, of making oneself easy to support. With high mobility and almost no personal cares, monks are able to devote most of their time and energy to their work, whether for their individual perfection or for the social good.

> "The monk is content with sufficient robes to protect the body and sufficient alms food for his body's needs. Wherever he may go he takes just these with him, just as a bird on the wing, wherever it may fly, flies only with the load of its wings."[3]

Thus, it is contentment and paucity of wishes accompanied by commitment to the development of the good and the abandonment of evil that are praised. Even contentment and paucity of wishes are to be qualified, that is, they must be accompanied by effort and diligence, not by complacency and idleness. The monk contents himself with whatever he gets so that he can devote more of his time and energy to his own personal development and the welfare of others. In other words, while it may be good for a monk to gain many possessions, it is not good to own or to hoard them. It is good rather to gain much, and give much away.

> "Furthermore, monks, he is content with whatever necessities, be it robes, alms food, shelter or medicines, he obtains. Furthermore, monks, he is continually stirring up effort to eliminate bad qualities, making dogged and vigorous progress in good things, and never throwing off his obligations."[4]

* * *

> "One is the road that leads to wealth, another the road that leads to Nibbāna. If a monk, disciple of the Buddha, has learned this, he will yearn not for honor, but will foster solitude."[5]

For the laity, as mentioned above, there is no instance in which poverty is encouraged. On the contrary, many passages in the Scriptures exhort lay people to seek and amass wealth in rightful ways. Among the good results of good *kamma*, one is to be wealthy.[6] What is blamed in connection with wealth is to earn it in dishonest ways. Worthy of blame also is the one who, having earned wealth, becomes enslaved by it and creates suffering as a result of it. No less evil and blameworthy than the unlawful earning of wealth is to accumulate riches out of stinginess, and not to spend it for the benefit and well-being of oneself, one's dependents, or other people. Again, squandering wealth foolishly or indulgently, or using it to cause suffering to other people, is also criticized:

> "Monks, if people knew, as I know, the fruits of sharing gifts, they would not enjoy their use without sharing them, nor would the taint of stinginess obsess the heart. Even if it were their last bit, their last morsel of food, they would not enjoy its use without sharing it if there was someone else to share it with."[7]

Good and praiseworthy wealthy people are those who seek wealth in rightful ways and use it for the good and happiness of both themselves and others. Accordingly, many of the Buddha's lay disciples, being wealthy, liberally devoted much or most of their wealth to the support of the sangha and to the alleviation of poverty and suffering. For example, the millionaire Anāthapiṇḍika is said in the Commentary on the Dhammapada to have spent a large amount of money every day to feed hundreds of monks as well as hundreds of the poor. Of course, in an ideal society, under an able and righteous ruler or under a righteous and effective administration, there would be no poor people, as all people would be at least self-sufficient, and monks would be the only community set apart to be sustained by the material surplus of the lay society.

Thus, contrary to the popular image of Buddhism as a religion of austerity, Buddhist teachings do acknowledge the role of material comfort in the creation of happiness. However, Buddhism aims at the development of human potential and, in this regard, material wealth is considered secondary. A lucrative economic activity that is conducive to well-being can contribute to human development—the accumulation of wealth for its own sake cannot.

Right Livelihood

Right Livelihood is one factor on the Noble Eightfold Path. It is not determined by the amount of material wealth it produces, but rather by the well-being it generates. Many livelihoods which produce a surplus of wealth simply cater to desires rather than providing for any true need.

For the individual, the objective of livelihood is to acquire the four necessities or requisites of human existence: food, clothing, shelter, and medicine. Again, the acquisition of these four requisites, be it in sufficient amount or in surplus, is not the ultimate objective. The four requisites are merely a foundation upon which efforts to realize higher objectives can be based.

Some people are content with few possessions and need only a minimum to devote their energies to mental and spiritual development. Others cannot live happily on such a small amount; they are more dependent on material goods. As long as their livelihood does not exploit others, however, Buddhism does not condemn their wealth. Moreover, people who are charitably inclined can use their wealth in ways that are beneficial for society as a whole.

In opposition to contemporary urban values, Buddhism does not measure a person's or nation's worth by material wealth. Nor does it go to the opposite extreme, as do Marxist thinkers, and condemn the accumulation of wealth as an evil in and of itself. Instead, Buddhism judges the ethical value of wealth by the ways in which it is obtained, and the uses to which it is put.

Miserliness

Obtaining wealth in immoral ways and using it to harmful ends are two evils associated with wealth. A third is hoarding wealth — refusing to either share one's wealth or put it to good use. In this story, the Buddha recounts the evils of miserliness:

At one time, King Pasenadi of Kosala visited the Buddha. The King told the Buddha that a rich old miser had recently died leaving no heir to his huge fortune, and the King had gone to oversee the transfer of the miser's wealth into the kingdom's treasury.

King Pasenadi described the amount of wealth he had to haul away: eight million gold coins, not to mention the silver ones, which were innumerable. And, he said, when the old miser was alive he had lived on broken rice and vinegar, dressed in three coarse cloths sewn together, used a broken-down chariot for transport and shaded himself with a sunshade made of leaves.

The Buddha remarked:

> "That is how it is, Your Majesty. The foolish man, obtaining fine requisites, supports neither himself nor his dependents, his father and mother, wife and children, his servants and employees, his friends and associates, in comfort. He does not make offerings, which are of great fruit, and which are conducive to mental well-being,

happiness and heaven, to religious mendicants. That wealth unconsumed and unused by him is confiscated by Kings, stolen by thieves, burnt by fire, swept aside by floods, or inherited by unfavored relatives. His wealth, accumulated and not used, disappears to no purpose. His wealth is like a forest pool, clear, cool and fresh, with good approaches and shady setting, in a forest of ogres. No-one can drink, bathe in or make use of that water.

"As for the wise man, having obtained fine requisites, he supports himself, his mother and father, his wife and children, his servants and employees, and his friends and associates comfortably, sufficiently. He makes offerings, which are of great fruit, and which are conducive to mental well-being, happiness and heaven, to religious mendicants. The wealth that he has so rightly used is not confiscated by Kings, thieves cannot steal it, fire cannot burn it, floods cannot carry it away, unfavored relatives cannot appropriate it. The wealth rightly used by him is put to use, it does not disappear in vain. His wealth is like a forest pool not far from a village or town, with cool, clear, fresh water, good approaches and shady setting. People can freely drink of that water, carry it away, bathe in it, or use it as they please.

"The evil person, obtaining wealth, neither uses it nor lets others use it, like a forest pool in a haunted forest—the water cannot be drunk and nobody dares to use it. The wise man, obtaining wealth, both uses it and puts it to use. Such a person is exemplary, he supports his relatives and is blameless. He attains to heaven."[8]

* * *

"Your Majesty, those people who, having obtained vast wealth, are not intoxicated by it, are not led into heedlessness and reckless indulgence which endangers others, are very rare in this world. Those who, having obtained much wealth, are intoxicated by it, led into heedlessness and reckless indulgence which endangers others, are truly of far greater number."[9]

Elsewhere in the Scriptures, the miserly person is likened to a bird called the "mayhaka" bird, which lives in the fig tree. While all the other birds flock to the tree and eat its fruits, all the mayhaka bird can do is stand there calling out "*mayhaṁ, mayhaṁ*" ("mine, mine").[10]

To sum up, harmful actions associated with wealth can appear in three forms: seeking wealth in dishonest or unethical ways; hoarding wealth for its own sake; and using wealth in ways that are harmful.

Knowing Wealth's Limitations

Wealthy people with virtue use their wealth to perform good works for themselves and others, but the truly wise also understand that wealth alone cannot make them free. In the passages below, the Buddha expounds on the limitations of wealth and exhorts us to strive for that which is higher than material possessions.

> "Actions, knowledge, qualities, morality and an ideal life: these are the gauges of a being's purity, not wealth or name."[11]

* * *

> "I see beings in this world who are wealthy: instead of sharing their wealth around, they become enslaved by it; they hoard it and demand more and more sensual gratification.
>
> "Kings conquer whole lands, reigning over realms that stretch from ocean to ocean, yet they are not content with simply this shore—they want the other side as well. Both Kings and ordinary people must die in the midst of want, never reaching an end to desire and craving. With craving unfulfilled, they cast off the body. There is no satisfying the desires for sense objects in this world.
>
> "Relatives let down their hair and grieve over deceased loved ones, wailing, 'Oh, our loved one has passed away from us.' They wrap the body in a cloth, set it upon the funeral pyre and cremate it; the undertakers take sticks and poke the body until it is wholly burnt. All the deceased can take with them is a single cloth, all wealth is left behind.
>
> "When it is time to die, no-one, neither relative nor friend, can forestall the inevitable. Possessions are carried off by the heirs while the deceased fares according to his kamma. When it is time to die, not one thing can you take with you, not even children, wife (or husband), wealth or land. Longevity cannot be obtained through

wealth, and old age cannot be bought off with it. The wise say that life is short, uncertain and constantly changing.

"Both the rich and the poor experience contact with the realm of senses; both the foolish and the wise experience contact also. But the foolish person, through lack of wisdom, is overwhelmed and stricken by it. As for the wise man, even though he experiences contact he is not upset. Thus, wisdom is better than wealth, because it leads to the highest goal in this life."[12]

Mental attitude to wealth

A true Buddhist lay person not only seeks wealth lawfully and spends it for constructive purposes, but also enjoys spiritual freedom, not being attached to it, infatuated with it or enslaved by it. This is the point where the mundane and the transcendent meet. The Buddha classifies lay people (*kāmabhogī*, those who partake in sense pleasures) into various levels according to lawful and unlawful means of seeking wealth, spending or not spending wealth for the happiness of oneself and others, and the attitude of greed and attachment or wisdom and spiritual freedom in dealing with wealth. The highest kind of person enjoys life on both the mundane and the transcendent planes as follows:

Mundane

1. Seeking wealth lawfully and honestly.
2. Seeing to one's own needs.
3. Sharing with others and performing meritorious deeds.

Transcendent

4. Making use of one's wealth without greed, longing or infatuation, heedful of the dangers and possessed of the insight that sustains spiritual freedom.

Such a person is said to be a Noble Disciple, one who is progressing toward individual perfection. Of particular note here is the compatibility between the mundane and the transcendent spheres of life, which combine to form the integral whole of Buddhist ethics, which is only perfected when the transcendent sphere is incorporated.

In spite of its great utility, then, too much importance should not be given to wealth. Its limitations in relation to the realization of the goal of *Nibbāna*, furthermore, should also be recognized. Though on the mundane level poverty is something to be avoided, a poor person is not completely deprived of means to do good for himself or society. The ten ways of making merit* may begin with giving, but they also include moral conduct, the development of mental qualities, the rendering of service, and the teaching of the Dhamma. Because of poverty, people may be too preoccupied with the struggle for survival to do anything for their own perfection, but when basic living needs are satisfied, if one is mentally qualified and motivated, there is no reason why one cannot realize individual perfection. While wealth as a resource for achieving social good can help create favorable circumstances for realizing individual perfection, ultimately it is mental maturity and wisdom, not wealth, that bring about its realization. Wealth mistreated and abused not only obstructs individual development, but can also be detrimental to the social good.

> "Wealth destroys the foolish, but not those who search for the Goal."[13]

A life that is free—one that is not overly reliant on material things—is a life that is not deluded by them. This demands a clear knowledge of the benefits and limitations of material possessions. Without such wisdom, we invest all our happiness in material things, even though they can never lead to higher qualities of mind. In fact, as long as we remain attached to them, possessions will hinder even simple peace of mind. By their very nature, material things lack the ability to completely satisfy: they are impermanent and unstable, they cannot be ultimately controlled and must inevitably go to dissolution. Clinging onto them, we suffer needlessly. When we were born they were not born with us, and when we die we cannot take them along.

* See Appendix

Used with wisdom, material goods can help relieve suffering, but used without wisdom, they only increase the burden. By consuming material goods with discrimination we can derive true value from them.

One who gains riches by diligent application to livelihood, and who puts that wealth to good use for himself and others, is said in Buddhism to be victorious in both this world and the next.[14] When he is also possessed of the wisdom that leads to detachment (*nissaraṇa-paññā*), when he neither becomes enslaved by possessions nor carries them as a burden, when he can live cheerfully and unconfused without being spoiled by worldly wealth, he is even more commendable.

The Major Characteristics of Buddhist Economics

1 Middle Way economics: realization of true well-being

Buddhism is full of teachings referring to the Middle Way, the right amount and knowing moderation, and all of these terms may be considered as synonyms for the idea of balance or equilibrium. Knowing moderation is referred to in the Buddhist scriptures as *mattaññutā*. Mattaññutā is the defining characteristic of Buddhist economics. Knowing moderation means knowing the optimum amount, how much is "just right." It is an awareness of that optimum point where the enhancement of true well-being coincides with the experience of satisfaction. This optimum point, or point of balance, is attained when we experience satisfaction at having answered the need for quality of life or well-being. Consumption, for example, which is attuned to the Middle Way, must be balanced to an amount appropriate to the attainment of well-being rather than the satisfaction of desires. Thus, in contrast to the classical economic equation of maximum consumption leading to maximum satisfaction, we have moderate, or wise consumption, leading to well-being.

2 *Middle Way economics: not harming oneself or others*

A further meaning of the term "just the right amount" is of not harming oneself or others. This is another important principle and one that is used in Buddhism as the basic criterion of human action, not only in relation to consumption, but for all human activity. Here it may be noted that in Buddhism "not harming others" applies not only to human beings but to all that lives.

From a Buddhist perspective, economic principles are related to the three interconnected aspects of human existence: human beings, society and the natural environment. Buddhist economics must be in concord with the whole causal process and to do that it must have a proper relationship with all three of those areas, and they in turn must be in harmony and mutually supportive. Economic activity must take place in such a way that it doesn't harm oneself (by causing a decline in the quality of life) and does not harm others (by causing problems in society or imbalance in the environment).

At the present time there is a growing awareness in developing countries of environmental issues. People are anxious about economic activities that entail the use of toxic chemicals and fossil fuels. Such activities are harmful to the health of individuals and to the welfare of society and the environment. They may be included in the phrase "harming oneself and harming others," and are a major problem for mankind.

Chapter Five

Teachings on Economics from the Buddhist Scriptures

The Buddhist teachings on economics are scattered throughout the Scriptures among teachings on other subjects. A teaching on mental training, for example, may include guidelines for economic activity, because in real life these things are all interconnected. Thus, if we want to find the Buddhist teachings on economics, we must extract them from teachings on other subjects.

Although the Buddha never specifically taught about the subject of economics, teachings about the four requisites— food, clothing, shelter and medicine—occur throughout the Pali Canon. In essence, all of the teachings concerning the four requisites are teachings on economics.

The Monastic Order

The Books of Discipline for the Monastic Order stipulate the attitude and conduct Buddhist monks and nuns are to adopt toward the four requisites. As mendicants, monks and nuns depend entirely on donations for their material needs. The Discipline lays down guidelines for a blameless life that is worthy of the support of the laity. A life dedicated to Dhamma study, meditation and teaching is Right Livelihood for monks and nuns.

The Discipline also contains standards and regulations for ensuring that the four requisites, once supplied to the Order, will be consumed in peace and harmony rather than contention and strife. Buddhist monks are forbidden from demanding special food or requisites. A monk must be content with little. In this passage, the Buddha instructs monks on the proper attitudes toward the four requisites.

> A monk in this Teaching and Discipline is one content with whatever robes he is given and praises contentment with whatever robes are given. He does not greedily seek robes in unscrupulous ways. If he does not obtain a robe, he is not vexed; if he obtains a robe, he is not attached, not enamored of it and not pleased over it. He uses that robe with full awareness of its benefits and its dangers. He has wisdom which frees him from attachment. Moreover, he does not exalt himself or disparage others on account of his contentment with whatever robes are offered. Any monk who is diligent, ardent, not given to laziness, who is fully aware and recollected in contentment with robes, is said to be stationed in the time-honored lineage.
>
> Moreover, a monk is content with whatever alms food he is given ...
>
> Moreover, a monk is content with whatever dwellings he is given ...
>
> Moreover, a monk is one who delights in developing skillful qualities and praises their development; he delights in abandoning unskillful qualities and praises their abandoning; he does not exalt himself nor disparage others on account of his delighting in skillful qualities and praising their development, nor on account of his abandoning of unskillful qualities and praising their abandoning. A monk who is diligent, ardent, not given to laziness, but fully aware and recollected in such development (*bhāvanā*) and abandoning (*pahāna*) is said to be stationed in the time-honored lineage.[1]

This passage shows the relationship between contentment with material possessions and effort—material requisites are used as a foundation for human development.

The monastic discipline exemplifies a life-style which makes use of the least possible amount of material goods. This is partly for practical reasons, to enable the Order to live in a way that does not overtax the community, and partly so that the monks can devote as much of their time and energy as possible in the study, practice and teaching of the Dhamma. It also enables them to live a life that is as independent of the social mainstream as possible, so that their livelihood is not at all geared to any socially valued gain. All Buddhist monks, be they *Arahants* (completely enlightened beings) or newly ordained monks, live their lives according to this same basic principle of a minimal amount of material possessions and an optimum of devotion to Dhamma practice.

To live happily without an abundance of material possessions, monks rely on *sīla*, morality or good conduct. Note that each of the four types of good conduct mentioned below[2] calls upon another spiritual quality to perfect it:

> Restraint of behavior (*pāṭimokkha saṁvara sīla*) means to live within the restraint of the Monastic Code of Discipline (*Pāṭimokkha*); to refrain from that which is forbidden, and to practise according to that which is specified, to diligently follow in all the training rules. This kind of *sīla* is perfected through *saddhā*, faith.
>
> Restraint of the senses (*indriya saṁvara sīla*) is accomplished by guarding over the mind so as not to let unskillful conditions, such as like, dislike, attachment or aversion, overwhelm it when experiencing any of the six kinds of sense impressions: sight, sound, smell, taste, sensation in the body or thought in the mind. This kind of *sīla* is perfected through *sati*, mindfulness or recollection.
>
> Purity of livelihood (*ājīva pārisuddhi sīla*) demands that one conduct one's livelihood honestly, avoiding ways of livelihood that are wrong. For a monk, this includes not bragging about

superhuman attainments, such as meditation accomplishments or stages of enlightenment, or asking for special food when one is not sick; refraining from extortion, such as putting on a display of austerity to impress people into giving offerings; not fawning or sweet talking supporters; not hinting or making signs to get householders to make offerings; not threatening them or bullying them into making offerings; and not bartering with them, such as in giving something little and expecting much in exchange. This kind of *sīla*, or purity, is perfected through *viriya*, effort.

Morality connected with requisites (*paccaya sannisita sīla*) means using the four requisites with circumspection, with an awareness of their true use and value, rather than using them out of desire. At meal time, this means eating food for the sake of good health, so that one is able to live comfortably enough to practise the Dhamma conveniently, not eating to indulge in the sensual pleasure of eating. This kind of *sīla* is perfected through *paññā*, wisdom.

Householders

While much of the Buddha's teachings were directed towards monks, there is no indication anywhere in the Scriptures that the Buddha wanted householders to live like monks. Nor is there any indication that the Buddha wanted everybody to become monks and nuns. In establishing the order of monks and nuns, the Buddha created an independent community as an example of righteousness, a community that could nourish society with the Dhamma and provide a refuge for those who wished to live a life dedicated to Dhamma study.

Within this community there are both formal members and true members. The formal members are those who are ordained into the Buddhist Order as monks and nuns and who live superimposed, as it were, onto normal "householder society." The truly free members, however, are those of the Noble Order, both ordained and householders, who have experienced transcendent insight and are scattered throughout the regular society of unenlightened beings.

While the teachings in the Books of Discipline can be applied to the lives of householders, they are more directly related to monks. The monastic life is designed to be comfortable even when the four requisites are in low supply. In this regard, monks and nuns serve as living examples that life can be happy and fulfilling even when the four requisites are not plentiful.

Most lay people, however, see the four requisites as a basis on which to build more wealth and comfort. While householders may seem to require more material goods than monks and nuns because of their demanding responsibilities, such as raising children and running a business, the fact remains that all of life's basic needs can be met by the four requisites.

Practical teachings on economic matters for householders are contained in the Books of Discourses, or Suttas. The Suttas recount the advice the Buddha gave to various people in various stations throughout his life. In the Suttas, the Buddha stresses four areas in which householders may relate skillfully to wealth:[3]

Acquisition—Wealth should not be acquired by exploitation, but through effort and intelligent action; it should be acquired in a morally sound way.

Safekeeping—Wealth should be saved and protected as an investment for the further development of livelihood and as an insurance against future adversity. When accumulated wealth exceeds these two needs, it may be used for creating social benefit by supporting community works.

Use—Wealth should be put to the following uses: 1) to support oneself and one's family; 2) to support the interests of fellowship and social harmony, such as in receiving guests, or in activities of one's friends or relatives; 3) to support good works, such as community welfare projects.

Mental attitude—Wealth should not become an obsession, a cause for worry and anxiety. It should rather be related to with an understanding of its true benefits and limitations, and dealt with in a way that leads to personal development.

The Buddha praised only those wealthy people who have obtained their wealth through their own honest labor and used it wisely, to beneficial ends. That is, the Buddha praised the quality of goodness and benefit more than wealth itself. The common tendency (in Thailand) to praise people simply because they are rich, based on the belief that their riches are a result of accumulated merit from previous lives, without due consideration of the factors from the present life, contradicts the teachings of Buddhism on two counts: Firstly, it does not exemplify the Buddha's example of praising goodness above wealth; secondly it does not make use of reasoned consideration of the entire range of factors involved.

The present life is much more immediate and as such must be afforded more importance. Previous *kamma* determines the conditions of one's birth, including physical attributes, talents, intelligence and certain personality traits. While it is said to be a determining factor for people who are born into wealthy families, the Buddha did not consider birth into a wealthy family as such to be worthy of praise, and Buddhism does not place much importance on birth station. The Buddha might praise the good *kamma* which enabled a person to attain such a favorable birth, but since their birth into a wealthy station is the fruition of good past *kamma*, such people have been duly rewarded and it is not necessary to praise them further.

A favorable birth is said to be a good capital foundation which affords some people better opportunities than others. As for the unfolding of the present life, the results of previous *kamma* stop at birth, and a new beginning is made. A good "capital foundation" can easily degenerate. If it is used with care and intelligence it will lead to benefit for all concerned, but if one is deluded by one's capital foundation, or favorable situation, one will use it in a way that not only wastes one's valuable opportunities, but leads to harm for all concerned. The important question for Buddhism is how people use their initial capital. The Buddha did not praise or criticize wealth; he was concerned with actions.

According to the Buddhist teachings, wealth should be used for the purpose of helping others; it should support a life of good conduct and human development. According to this principle, when wealth arises for one person, the whole of society benefits, and although it belongs to one person, it is just as if it belonged to the whole community. A wealthy person who uses wealth in this manner is likened to a fertile field in which rice grows abundantly for the benefit of all. Such people generate great benefit for those around them. Without them, the wealth they create would not come to be, and neither would the benefit resulting from it. Guided by generosity, these people feel moved to represent the whole of society, and in return they gain the respect and trust of the community to use their wealth for beneficial purposes.

The Buddha taught that a householder who shares his wealth with others is following the path of the Noble Ones:

> "If you have little, give little; if you own a middling amount, give a middling amount; if you have much, give much. It is not fitting not to give at all. Kosiya, I say to you, 'Share your wealth, use it. Tread the path of the noble ones. One who eats alone eats not happily.'"[4]

Some people adhere to the daily practice of not eating until they have given something to others. This practice was adopted by a reformed miser in the time of the Buddha, who said, "As long as I have not first given to others each day, I will not even drink water."[5]

When the wealth of a virtuous person grows, other people stand to gain. But the wealth of a mean person grows at the expense of misery for those around him. People who get richer and richer while society degenerates and poverty spreads are using their wealth wrongly. Such wealth does not fulfil its true function. It is only a matter of time before something breaks down—either the rich, or the society, or both, must go. The community may strip the wealthy of their privileges and redistribute the wealth in the hands of new "stewards," for better or for worse. If people use wealth wrongly, it ceases to be a benefit and becomes a bane, destroying human dignity, individual welfare and the community.

Buddhism stresses that our relationship with wealth be guided by wisdom and a clear understanding of its true value and limitations. We should not be burdened or enslaved by it. Rather, we should be masters of our wealth and use it in ways that are beneficial to others. Wealth should be used to create benefit in society, rather than contention and strife. It should be spent in ways that relieve problems and lead to happiness rather than to tension, suffering and mental disorder.

Here is a passage from the Scriptures illustrating the proper Buddhist attitude to wealth:

> "Bhikkhus, there are these three groups of people in this world. What are the three? They are the blind, the one-eyed, and the two-eyed.
>
> "Who is the blind person? There are some in this world who do not have the vision which leads to acquisition of wealth or to the increase of wealth already gained. Moreover, they do not have the vision which enables them to know what is skillful and what is unskillful ... what is blameworthy and what is not ... what is coarse and what is refined ... good and evil. This is what I mean by one who is blind.
>
> "And who is the one-eyed person? Some people in this world have the vision which leads to the acquisition of wealth, or to the increase of wealth already obtained, but they do not have the vision that enables them to know what is skillful and what is not ... what is blameworthy and what is not ... what is coarse and what is refined ... good and evil. This I call a one-eyed person.
>
> "And who is the two-eyed person? Some people in this world possess both the vision that enables them to acquire wealth and to capitalize on it, and the vision that enables them to know what is skillful and what is not ... what is blameworthy and what is not ... what is coarse and what is refined ... good and evil. This I call one with two eyes ...
>
> "One who is blind is hounded by misfortune on two counts: he has no wealth, and he performs no good works. The second kind of

person, the one-eyed, looks about for wealth irrespective of whether it is right or wrong. It may be obtained through theft, cheating, or fraud. He enjoys pleasures of the senses obtained from his ability to acquire wealth, but as a result he goes to hell. The one eyed person suffers according to his deeds.

"The two eyed person is a fine human being, one who shares out a portion of the wealth obtained through his diligent labor. He has noble thoughts, a resolute mind, and attains to a good bourn, free of suffering. Avoid the blind and the one-eyed, and associate with the two-eyed."[6]

Government

The Buddha said "poverty is suffering in this world."[7] Here he speaks to the use of wealth by governments. Poverty and want, like greed (to which they are closely related) contribute to crime and social discontent.[8] Buddhism maintains that it is the duty of the government or the administrators of a country to see to the needs of those who are in want and to strive to banish poverty from the land. At the very least, honest work should be available to all people, trade and commerce should be encouraged, capital should be organized and industries monitored to guard against dishonest or exploitive practices. By this criteria, the absence of poverty is a better gauge of a government's success than the presence of millionaires.

It is often asked which economic or political system is most compatible with Buddhism. Buddhism does not answer such a question directly. One might say Buddhism would endorse whatever system is most compatible with it, but economic and political systems are a question of method, and methods, according to Buddhism, should be attuned to time and place.

What is the purpose of a government's wealth? Essentially, a government's wealth is for the purpose of supporting and organizing its citizens' lives in the most efficient and beneficial way possible. Wealth enables us to practise and to attain progressively higher levels of well-being. Wealth should support the community in such a way that people who live in it conduct good lives and are motivated to a higher good.

A political or economic system that uses wealth to these ends is compatible with Buddhism (subject to the stipulation that it is a voluntary or free system rather than an authoritarian one). Specific systems are simply methods dependent on time and place, and can vary accordingly. For example, when the Buddha established the Order of monks as a specialized community, he set up rules limiting a monk's personal possessions. Most requisites were to be regarded as communal property of the Order.

The Buddha gave different teachings regarding wealth for householders or worldly society. In his day, there were two main political systems in India: some parts of the country were ruled by absolute monarchies, others were ruled by republican states. The Buddha gave separate teachings for each. This is characteristic of his teachings. Buddhism is not a religion of ideals and philosophy, but a religion of practice. The Buddha made his teaching applicable to the real life of the people in the society of the time.

If the Buddha had waited until he had designed a perfect society before he taught, he would have fallen into idealism and romanticism. Since the perfect society will always be a "hoped-for" society, the Buddha gave teachings that could be put to effect in the present time, or, in his words, "those truths which are truly useful."

For the monarchies, the Buddha taught the duties of a Wheel-Turning Emperor, exhorting rulers to use their absolute power as a tool for generating benefit in the community rather than a tool for seeking personal happiness. For the republican states, he taught the *aparihāniyadhamma**—principles and methods for encouraging social harmony and preventing decline. In their separate ways, both these teaching show how a people can live happily under different political systems.

---

* See Appendix

When the absolute monarchy reached its highest perfection in India, the Emperor Ashoka used these Buddhist principles to govern his empire. He wrote in the Edicts, "His Highness, Priyadassī, loved by the devas, does not see rank or glory as being of much merit, except if that rank or glory is used to realize the following aim: 'Both now and in the future, may the people listen to my teaching and practise according to the principles of Dhamma.'"[9]

The ideal society is not one in which all people occupy the same station; such a society is in fact not possible. The ideal society is one in which human beings, training themselves in mind and intellect, although possessing differences, are nevertheless striving for the same objectives. Even though they are different they live together harmoniously. At the same time, it is a society which has a noble choice, a noble way out, for those so inclined, in the form of a religious life. (Even in the society of the future Buddha, Sri Ariya Metteyya, where everyone is said to be equal, there is still to be found the division of monks and laypeople.)

While absolute equality is impossible, governments should ensure that the four requisites are distributed so all citizens have enough to live on comfortably and can find honest work. Moreover, the economic system in general should lead to a harmonious community rather than to contention and strife, and material possessions used as a base for beneficial human development rather than as an end in themselves.

In one Sutta, the Buddha admonishes the Universal Emperor to apportion some of his wealth to the poor. The emperor is told to watch over his subjects and prevent abject poverty from arising.[10] Here we see that ethical economic management for a ruler or governor is determined by the absence of poverty in his domain, rather than by a surplus of wealth in his coffers or in the hands of a select portion of the population. When this basic standard is met, the teachings do not prohibit the accumulation of wealth or stipulate that it should be distributed equally.

With an understanding of the Buddhist perspective on social practice, those involved in such matters can debate which system is most compatible with Buddhism. Or they may opt to devise a new, more effective system. This might be the best alternative. However, it is a matter of practical application which is beyond the scope of this book.

The inner perspective

The Abhidhamma Piṭaka contains the Buddha's more esoteric teachings. While the Abhidhamma does not directly address economics, it does have a strong indirect connection because it analyses the mind and its constituents in minute detail. These mental factors are the root of all human behavior, including, of course, economic activity. Negative mental constituents such as greed, aversion, delusion and pride motivate economic activity as do the positive constituents such as non-greed, non-aversion and non-delusion, faith, generosity, and goodwill. In this respect, the Abhidhamma is a study of economics on its most fundamental level.

In a similar connection, the more esoteric practices of Buddhism, meditation in particular, relate indirectly but fundamentally to economics. Through meditation and mental training, we come to witness the stream of causes and conditions that begin as mental conditions and lead to economic activity. With this insight, we can investigate our mental process and make sound ethical judgements. Meditation helps us to see how ethical and unethical behavior are the natural consequence of the mental conditions which motivate them. Individual people, classes, races and nationalities are neither intrinsically good nor evil. It is rather our mental qualities that guide our behavior toward the ethical and the unethical. Greed, hatred and delusion drive us to unethical acts. Wisdom and a desire for true well-being guide us to ethical behavior and a good life.

With meditation, we gain perspective on our motivations; we sharpen our awareness and strengthen free will. Thus, when it comes to making economic decisions, decision about our livelihood and consumption, we can better resist compulsions driven by fear, craving, and pride and choose instead a moral course that aims at true well-being. In this way, we begin to see how mental factors form the basis of all economic matters, and we realize that the development of this kind of mental discernment leads the way to true economic and human development.

Perhaps more importantly, through meditation training it is possible to realize a higher kind of happiness—inner peace, the independent kind of happiness. When we have the ability to find peace within ourselves we can use wealth, which is no longer necessary for our own happiness, freely for the social good.

Seeking and protecting wealth

The following Sutta offers teachings on livelihood for a householder with an emphasis on the benefits that arise from right livelihood.

At one time, the Brahmin Ujjaya went to visit the Buddha to ask his advice on how to gain prosperity through right livelihood. The Buddha answered by explaining the conditions that would lead to happiness in the present and in the future:

> "Brahmin, these four conditions lead to happiness and benefit in the present. They are, industriousness, watchfulness, good company and balanced livelihood.
>
> "And what is the endowment of industriousness (*uṭṭhānasampadā*)? A son of good family supports himself through diligent effort. Be it through farming, commerce, raising livestock, a military career, or the arts, he is diligent, he applies himself, and he is skilled. He is not lazy in his work, but clever, interested. He knows how to manage his work, he is able and responsible: this is called the endowment of industriousness.
>
> "And what is the endowment of watchfulness (*ārakkhasampadā*)? A son of good family has wealth, the fruit of his own sweat and labor, rightly obtained by him. He applies himself to protecting that wealth, thinking, 'How can I prevent this wealth from being confis-

cated by the King, stolen by thieves, burnt by fire, swept away by floods or appropriated by unfavored relatives?' This is called the endowment of watchfulness.

"And what is good company (*kalyāṇamittatā*)? Herein, a son of good family, residing in a town or village, befriends, has discourse with, and seeks advice from, those householders, sons of householders, young people who are mature and older people who are venerable, who are possessed of faith, morality, generosity, and wisdom. He studies and emulates the faith of those with faith; he studies and emulates the morality of those with morality; he studies and emulates the generosity of those who are generous; he studies and emulates the wisdom of those who are wise. This is to have good company.

"And what is balanced livelihood (*samajīvitā*)? A son of good family supports himself in moderation, neither extravagantly nor stintingly. He knows the causes of increase and decrease of wealth, he knows which undertakings will yield an income higher than the expenditure rather than the expenditure exceeding the income. Like a person weighing things on a scale, he knows the balance either way ... If this young man had only a small income but lived extravagantly, it could be said of him that he consumed his wealth as if it were peanuts. If he had a large income but used it stintingly, it could be said of him that he will die like a pauper. But because he supports himself in moderation, it is said that he has balanced livelihood.

"Brahmin, the wealth rightly gained in this way has four pathways of decline. They are to be given to debauchery, drink, gambling, and association with evil friends. It is like a large reservoir with four channels going into it and four channels going out. If the channels going inward are closed off, and the channels going out opened up, and the rain does not fall in due season, that large reservoir can be expected only to decrease, not to increase ...

"Brahmin, wealth so gained rightly has four pathways of prosperity. They are to refrain from debauchery, drink and gambling, and to associate with good friends, to be drawn to good people. It is like a large reservoir with four channels leading into it and four channels leading out. If the channels leading into it are opened up, and the channels leading out are closed off, and rain falls in due season, it can be expected that for this reservoir there will be only increase, not decrease ... Brahmin, these four conditions are for the happiness and benefit of a young man in the present moment."[11]

The Buddha then went on to describe four conditions which lead to happiness and benefit in the future. In short, they are to possess the spiritual qualities of faith, morality, generosity and wisdom.

The Happiness of a Householder

The following teaching was given to the merchant Anāthapiṇḍika. It is known simply as the four kinds of happiness for a householder:

"Herein, householder, these four kinds of happiness are appropriate for one who leads the household life and enjoys the pleasures of the senses. They are the happiness of ownership, the happiness of enjoyment, the happiness of freedom from debt, and the happiness of blamelessness.

"What is the happiness of ownership (*atthisukha*)? A son of good family possesses wealth that has been obtained by his own diligent labor, acquired through the strength of his own arms and the sweat of his own brow, rightly acquired, rightly gained. He experiences pleasure, he experiences happiness, thinking, 'I possess this wealth that has been obtained by my own diligent labor, acquired through the strength of my own arms and the sweat of my own brow, rightly acquired, rightly gained.' This is the happiness of ownership.

"And what is the happiness of enjoyment (*bhogasukha*)? Herein, a son of good family consumes, puts to use, and derives benefit from the wealth that has been obtained by his own diligent labor, acquired through the strength of his own arms and the sweat of his own brow, rightly acquired, rightly gained. He experiences pleasure, he experiences happiness, thinking, 'Through this wealth that has been obtained by my own diligent labor, acquired through the strength of my own arms and the sweat of my own brow, rightly acquired, rightly gained, I have derived benefit and performed good works.' This is called the happiness of enjoyment.

"And what is the happiness of freedom from debt (*anaṇasukha*)?

Herein, a son of good family owes no debt, be it great or small, to anyone at all. He experiences pleasure and happiness, reflecting, 'I owe no debts, be they great or small, to anyone at all.' This is called the happiness of freedom from debt.

"And what is the happiness of blamelessness (*anavajjasukha*)? Herein, a noble disciple is possessed of blameless bodily actions, blameless speech, and blameless thoughts. He experiences pleasure and happiness, thinking, 'I am possessed of blameless bodily actions, blameless speech, and blameless thoughts.' This is called the happiness of blamelessness.

"When he realizes the happiness of being free from debt, he is in a position to appreciate the happiness of owning possessions. As he uses his possessions, he experiences the happiness of enjoyment. Clearly seeing this, the wise man, comparing the first three kinds of happiness with the last, sees that they are not worth a sixteenth part of the happiness that arises from blameless behavior."[12]

The Benefits of wealth

In this passage, the Buddha explains to the merchant Anāthapiṇḍika some of the benefits that can arise from wealth. Since the teachings are specific to an earlier time, the reader is advised to glean the gist of them and apply it to the modern day:

"Herein, householder, there are five uses to which wealth can be put. They are:

"With the wealth that has been obtained by his own diligent labor, acquired through the strength of his own arms and the sweat of his own brow, rightly acquired, rightly gained, the noble disciple supports himself comfortably, sufficiently, he applies himself to seeing to his own happiness in rightful ways. He supports his father and mother ... wife and children, servants and workers comfortably, to a sufficiency, applying himself to their needs and their happiness as is proper. This is the first benefit to be obtained from wealth.

"Moreover, with the wealth that has been obtained by his own diligent labor, acquired through the strength of his own arms and the sweat of his own brow, rightly acquired, rightly gained, the noble disciple supports his friends and associates comfortably, to a sufficiency, taking an interest in their happiness as is proper. This is the second benefit to be derived from wealth.

"Moreover, with the wealth that has been obtained by his own diligent labor, acquired through the strength of his own arms and the sweat of his own brow, rightly acquired, rightly gained, the noble disciple protects his wealth from the dangers of confiscation by kings, theft, fire, flood, and appropriation by unfavored relatives. He sees to his own security. This is the third benefit to be derived from wealth.

"Moreover, with the wealth that has been obtained by his own diligent labor, acquired through the strength of his own arms and the sweat of his own brow, rightly acquired, rightly gained, the noble disciple makes the five kinds of sacrifice. They are: to relatives (supporting relatives); to visitors (receiving guests); to ancestors (offerings made in the name of ancestors); to the king (for taxes and public works); and to the gods (that is, he supports religion). This is another benefit to be derived from wealth.

"Moreover, with the wealth that has been obtained by his own diligent labor, acquired through the strength of his own arms and the sweat of his own brow, rightly acquired, rightly gained, the noble disciple makes offerings which are of the highest merit, which are conducive to mental well-being, happiness and heaven, to religious mendicants, those who live devoted to heedfulness, are established in patience and gentleness, are trained, calmed, and cooled of defilements. This is the fifth benefit to be obtained from wealth.

"Householder, there are these five benefits to be obtained from wealth. If wealth is used by a noble disciple in such a way that these five benefits are fulfilled, and if it should then become spent, that noble disciple can reflect thus: 'Whatever benefit is to be obtained from wealth, I have obtained. Now my wealth is spent.' That noble disciple experiences no distress on that account. And if, after that noble disciple has used his wealth to provide these five benefits, that wealth should increase, that noble disciple reflects thus: 'Whatever benefit is to be obtained from my wealth I have already obtained. And now my wealth has increased.' That noble disciple is also not distressed on that account; he is distressed in neither case."[13]

Wealth and spiritual development

The Buddha taught that basic material needs must be met before spiritual development can begin. The following story[14] illustrates how hunger is both a cause of physical suffering and an obstacle to spiritual progress:

One morning while the Buddha was residing in the Jetavana monastery near the city of Sāvatthī, he sensed with his psychic powers that the spiritual faculties of a certain poor peasant living near the city of Āḷavī were mature enough for him to understand the teachings, and that he was ripe for enlightenment. So, later that morning, the Buddha set off walking to Āḷavī, some 30 *yojanas* (about 48 km) away.

The inhabitants of Āḷavī held the Buddha in great respect, and on his arrival warmly welcomed him. Eventually a place was prepared for everyone to gather together and listen to a discourse. However, as the Buddha's particular purpose in going to Āḷavī was to enlighten this one poor peasant, he waited for him to arrive before starting to talk.

The peasant heard the news of the Buddha's visit and, since he had been interested in the Buddha's teaching for some time, he decided to go to listen to the discourse. But it so happened that one of his cows had just disappeared and he wondered whether he should go and listen to the Buddha first and look for his cow afterwards, or to look for the cow first. He decided that he should look for the cow first and quickly set off into the forest to search for it. Eventually the peasant found his cow and drove it back to the herd, but by the time everything was as it should be, he was very tired. The peasant thought to himself, "Time is getting on, if I go back home first it will take up even more time. I'll just go straight into the city to listen to the Buddha's discourse." Having made up his mind, the poor peasant started walking into Āḷavī. By the time he arrived at the place set up for the talk, he was exhausted and very hungry.

When the Buddha saw the peasant's condition, he asked the city elders to arrange some food for the poor man, and only when the peasant had eaten his fill and was refreshed did the Buddha start to teach. While listening to the discourse the peasant realized the fruit of 'Stream Entry,' the first stage of enlightenment. The Buddha had fulfilled his purpose in travelling to Āḷavī.

After the talk was over, the Buddha bade farewell to the people of Āḷavī and set off back to the Jetavana monastery. During the walk back, the monks who were accompanying him started to discuss the day's events: "What was that all about? The Lord didn't quite seem himself today. I wonder why he got them to arrange food for the peasant like that, before he would agree to give his discourse."

The Buddha, knowing the subject of the monks' discussion, turned back towards them and started to explain his reasons, saying, "When people are overwhelmed and in pain through suffering, they are incapable of understanding religious teaching." The Buddha went on to say that hunger is the most severe of all illnesses and that conditioned phenomena provide the basis for the most ingrained suffering. Only when one understands these truths will one realize the supreme happiness of Nibbāna.

Buddhism considers economics to be of great significance—this is demonstrated by the Buddha having the peasant eat something before teaching him. Economists might differ as to whether the Buddha's investment of a 45 kilometer walk was worth the enlightenment of one single person, but the point is that not only is Right Livelihood one of the factors of the Eightfold Path, but that hungry people cannot appreciate the Dhamma. Although consumption and economic wealth are important, they are not goals in themselves, but are merely the foundations for human development and the enhancement of the quality of life. They allow us to realize the profound: after eating, the peasant listened to Dhamma and became enlightened. Buddhist economics ensures that the creation of wealth leads to a life in which people can develop their potentials and increase in goodness. Quality of life, rather than wealth for its own sake, is the goal.

Appendix

From the Scriptures

General

Two kinds of abundance (*vepulla*) A.I. 93

1. Abundance of material things
2. Abundance of virtues or knowledge

Two kinds of happiness (*sukha*) A.I. 80

1. Happiness dependent on material things
2. Happiness that is independent of material things; spiritual happiness

The eight worldly conditions (*lokadhamma*) A.IV. 157

1 Gain
2 Loss
3 Honor
4 Obscurity
5 Praise
6 Blame
7 Happiness
8 Suffering

Personal practice

Ten bases of meritorious action (*puññakiriyāvatthu*) D.A.III. 999; Comp. 146

1. Generosity
2. Morality
3. Mental development
4. Humility
5. Service
6. Sharing merit
7. Rejoicing in the merit of others
8. Listening to the True Teaching
9. Teaching the True Teaching
10. Straightening out one's views

Four virtues of a good householder (*gharāvāsa-dhamma*) S.I. 215; Sn. 189

1. Honesty
2. Self-discipline
3. Forbearance
4. Generosity

Four pathways to ruin (*abhāyamukha*) A.IV. 283

1. Debauchery
2. Drunkenness
3. Gambling
4. Bad company

Five kinds of wrongful trade (*vaṇijjā*) A.III. 207

1. Trade in weapons
2. Trade in human beings
3. Trade in flesh (animals for meat)
4. Trade in spirits (and drugs)
5. Trade in poison

The ten levels of householders (*kāmabhogī* – those who enjoy sense pleasures) S.IV. 331; A.V. 176

1. Those who seek wealth unlawfully, and in so doing provide happiness neither for themselves nor for others; they do not share it and they perform no meritorious deeds.
2. Those who seek wealth unlawfully, and in so doing provide happiness for themselves, but not for others; they do not share it and they perform no meritorious deeds.
3. Those who seek wealth unlawfully, and in so doing provide happiness for themselves; they share it with others and perform meritorious deeds.
4. Those who seek wealth both lawfully and unlawfully, and in so doing provide happiness neither for themselves nor for others; they do not share it and they perform no meritorious deeds.
5. Those who seek wealth both lawfully and unlawfully, and in so doing provide happiness for themselves, but not for others; they do not share it and they perform no meritorious deeds.
6. Those who seek wealth both lawfully and unlawfully, and in so doing provide happiness for themselves, share it with others and perform meritorious deeds.
7. Those who seek wealth lawfully, and in so doing provide happiness neither for themselves nor others; nor do they share it or perform meritorious deeds.
8. Those who seek wealth lawfully, and in so doing provide happiness for themselves, but not for others; they do not share it and they perform no meritorious deeds.
9. Those who seek wealth lawfully, and in so doing provide happiness for themselves and others; they share it and perform meritorious deeds—but they are still attached to and infatuated with their wealth, are heedless of its dangers, and lack the insight to achieve spiritual freedom.
10. Those who seek wealth lawfully, and in so doing provide happiness for themselves and others; they share it and perform meritorious deeds—moreover, they are not attached to or infatuated with their wealth, they are heedful of its dangers, and they possess the insight that leads to spiritual freedom.

On wealth

Fourfold division of wealth (*bhogavibhāga*) D.III. 188

1. One part to be used for conduct of daily life and fulfilling obligations
2–3. Two parts to be invested in expanding business enterprises
4. One part to be put aside for a rainy day

Five uses to which wealth can be put (*bhoga-ādiya*) A.III. 45

1. Comfortable support of oneself, one's family and dependents
2. Sharing with one's friends and associates
3. Investment against future misfortune
4. The fivefold offering
   a. To relatives
   b. To guests (in reception)
   c. To the departed (by dedicating merits)
   d. To the government (i.e., taxes etc.)
   e. To the deities (according to one's faith)
5. Support of spiritual teachers and virtuous monks

Five kinds of meanness (*macchariya*) D.III. 234; A.III. 271; Vbh. 357

1. Meanness as to dwelling place (begrudging a dwelling to others)
2. Meanness as to family (begrudging others' acquaintance with one's influential connections)
3. Meanness as to gain (begrudging or thwarting the gains of others)
4. Meanness as to recognition (begrudging recognition or praise given to others)
5. Meanness as to knowledge or abilities (not sharing one's knowledge with others)

Social

Four bases of social harmony (*saṅgahavatthu*) D.III. 152, 232; A.II. 32, 248; A.IV. 218, 363

1. Generosity

2. Kindly speech
3. Service
4. Participation

Four bases of social harmony for a king (*rāja-saṅgahavatthu*) S.I. 76; A.II. 42; IV. 151; It. 21; Sn. 303; S.A.I. 145; Sn.A. 321

1. Shrewdness in agriculture
2. Shrewdness in promotion of government officials
3. Skilful bestowal of favors
4. Kindly and pleasing speech

Five ways an employer/master should serve his employees/servants D.III. 189-192

1. By assigning them work in accordance with their capabilities
2. By giving them due wages
3. By providing care in times of sickness
4. By sharing occasional luxuries
5. By giving them holidays at suitable times

Five ways an employee/servant should serve his employer/master D.III. 189-192

1. By getting up before him to work
2. By finishing work after him
3. By taking only what is given
4. By doing his work well
5. By spreading the good reputation of his employer

The Seven Conditions for Community Welfare (aparihāniyadhamma) D.II. 73; A.IV. 15

1. To hold regular and frequent meetings
2. To meet together in harmony, disperse in harmony, and conduct business and duties in harmony
3. To introduce no new ordinances, to break up no established ordinances, but to abide by the original principles
4. To honer and respect the elders and listen to their counsel
5. To honor the womenfolk of the community, not to abuse them
6. To honor the shrines worshipped by the community and not to neglect

the ceremonies to be conducted for them

7. To provide rightful protection, shelter and support for the *Arahants* (enlightened beings) and to welcome them to the community

The ten Virtues or Duties of a king (*rājadhamma*) J.V. 378

1. Charity, generosity
2. Morality
3. Altruism
4. Honesty
5. Kindness
6. Self-control
7. Non-anger
8. Nonviolence
9. Forbearance
10. Uprightness

The Twelve Duties of a Universal Emperor (*cakkavatti-vatta*) D.III. 61

1 Rule by righteousness
Provision of ward and protection to
   2 Those in the Emperor's immediate circle
   3 The armed forces
   4 Governors and administrative officers
   5 Royal dependents, civil servants
   6 Brahmins, householders, craftsmen, traders
   7 Town and country dwellers
   8 Religious devotees
   9 Beasts and birds
10 Prevention of wrongdoing in the Kingdom
11 Distribution of wealth to the poor
12 Seeking advice from sages, aspiring to greater virtue

References

Chapter 2

1 Dh. 186
2 Dh. 251
3 S.I. 117
4 J.II 310

Chapter 3

1 From "*Economics '73–'74*," Various Contributors, 1973, The Dushkin Publishing Group, Inc., Guildford, Connecticut.
2 M.I. 10; Nd[1] 496
3 D.III. 214; A.I. 50, 95; Dhs. 8, 234
4 From "*Economics '73–'74*," Various Contributors, 1973, The Dushkin Publishing Group, Inc., Guildford, Connecticut.
5 A.I. 30
6 Vin.I. 9; S.V. 421; Vbh. 99

Chapter 4

1 A.III. 350
2 A.III. 352

3 A.II. 209
4 D.III. 226, 296; A.V. 23
5 Dh. 75
6 See, for example, A.II. 204 cf. the Cūlakammavibhaṅga Sutta in M.III.
7 It. 18
8 S.I. 89-91
9 S.I. 74
10 J.III. 299-302
11 M.III. 262; S.I. 34,55. It is said that by 'action' here is meant 'Right Action,' 'knowledge' is Right Thought and Right View, 'qualities' (dhamma) refers to the factors of samādhi, and morality refers to Right Speech and Right Livelihood.
12 M.II. 72-73; Thag. 776-784
13 Dh. 355
14 As in D.III. 181

Chapter Five

1 A.II. 27
2 Vism. 16; Comp. 212
3 D.III. 188; A.V. 176-182
4 J.V. 382
5 J.V. 393-411
6 A.I. 128
7 A.III. 351
8 D.III. 65, 70
9 Ashokan Edict No. 10.
10 Dhanānuppadāna—apportioning of some wealth to the poor—one of the twelve duties of a Universal Emperor D.III. 61
11 A.IV. 281
12 A.II. 69
13 A.III. 45
14 Dh.A.III. 262

Appendix

1 A.I. 93
2 A.I. 80
3 A.IV. 157
4 D.A.III. 999; Comp. 146
5 S.I. 215; Sn. 189

6 A.IV. 283
7 A.III. 207
8 S.IV. 331; A.V. 176
9 D.III. 188
10 A.III. 45
11 D.III. 234; A.III. 271; Vbh. 357
12 D.III. 152, 232; A.II. 32, 248; A.IV. 218, 363
13 S.I. 76; A.II. 42; IV. 151; It. 21; Sn. 303; S.A.I. 145; Sn.A. 321
14 D.III. 189-192
15 D.III. 189-192
16 D.II. 73; A.IV. 15
17 J.V. 378
18 D.III. 61

D. = Dīgha Nikāya (3 vols.)
A. = Aṅguttara Nikāya (5 vols.)
S. = Saṁyutta Nikāya (5 vols.)
Vin. = Vinaya Piṭaka (5 vols.)
Vism. = Visuddhimagga
Comp. = Compendium of Philosophy (Abhidhammatthasaṅgaha)

Sources

This book has been compiled from material in the following works by the author:

1. *Buddhist Economics*, the original booklet of a talk given by the author at Thammasat University on March 9, 1989; translated by Dhammavijaya.

2. "A way out of the Economic Bind on Thai Society" (*Tahng ork jahk rabop setthagit tee krorp ngum sungkhom thai*), published in Thai by the Buddhadhamma Foundation, translated by Bruce Evans.

3. Parts of the chapter called 'The Problem of Motivation,' translated by Bruce Evans from the book *Buddhadhamma*.

4. The section on Right Livelihood, which makes up part of the chapter on morality (sīla) from *Buddhadhamma*, translated by Bruce Evans.

5. Part of the chapter entitled "Foundations of Buddhist Social Ethics," written in English by the author, which appeared in *Ethics, Wealth and Salvation*, edited by Russell F. Sizemore and Donald K. Swearer, published by University of South Carolina Press, 1990, Colombia, S. Carolina.